S0-BFC-853

Understanding Education Indicators

A Practical Primer for Research and Policy

Understanding Education Indicators

A Practical Primer for Research and Policy

MIKE PLANTY
DEVEN CARLSON

Teachers College, Columbia University
New York and London

Published by Teachers College Press, 1234 Amsterdam Avenue, New York, NY 10027

Copyright © 2010 by Teachers College, Columbia University

All rights reserved. No part of this publication may be reproduced or transmitted in any form or by any means, electronic or mechanical, including photocopy, or any information storage and retrieval system, without permission from the publisher.

Library of Congress Cataloging-in-Publication Data

Planty, Mike.
    Understanding education indicators : a practical primer for research and policy / Mike Planty, Deven Carlson.
    p. cm.
    Includes bibliographical references and index.
    ISBN 978-0-8077-5120-6 (pbk.)
    1. Education indicators. 2. Educational statistics. I. Carlson, Deven. II. Title.
    LB2846.P55 2010
    370 2'1—dc22   2010013699

ISBN 978-0-8077-5120-6 (paperback)

Printed on acid-free paper
Manufactured in the United States of America

17   16   15   14   13   12   11   10   8   7   6   5   4   3   2   1

To Michelle, Sammy, and Charlie
—MP

To Nina
—DC

Contents

Preface

Why a book on education indicators and why one now? Our decision to undertake this book is driven by the current focus on accountability at all levels and sectors within the education system. This focus has resulted in our education system facing several new and unique pressures. For example, only in the last decade have elementary and secondary schools become accountable not only for achieving specific performance goals and preventing dropouts, but also for maintaining safe and healthy environments, employing a cadre of highly qualified teachers, and providing a challenging educational curriculum. Similarly, there is a nascent movement to increase accountability in postsecondary education. These pressures are fostered by the labor market's concern about America's position as an international competitor.

The pressures facing our education system are wide-ranging and diverse, but they share one commonality. Specifically, these pressures have increased the demand for, and emphasis placed on, indicators that purport to describe the state and progress of our education system. The increased reliance on indicators has occurred with the noblest of intentions and is, on balance, a positive development. It is often said that if something is not measured, you can never hope to change it. That being said, in this push to bring data to bear on all of the important education issues of the day, one simple, yet vitally important, fact is often overlooked: Not all indicators are created equal. Indicators employ data sources, measurement methods, and presentation styles that are of varying levels of quality.

The differing quality of indicators represents a potential problem because many consumers of education indicators are unaware of this variation. Most individuals take the information provided by indicators at face value, accepting or dismissing the information wholesale; rarely do people question or take a critical look at the process that produced the indicator. We hope this book will prompt individuals to take an informed look at indicator quality, and we provide a comprehensive framework for doing so. In particular, we introduce readers to the idea of *an indicator's error structure*, based on the concept of total survey error developed by Groves et al. (2004). The basic idea of indicator error is that any number of potential factors can cause an indicator to be imperfect. It is important to determine whether the imperfections undermine the purpose and intent of the indicator. Introducing readers to the issues and language of measurement, data, and basic statistics allows them to become educated consumers of the types and importance of indicator error. By drawing on the fields of social indicators—survey research, statistics, and education—we hope the reader walks away with a comprehensive interdisciplinary approach to understanding and evaluating the value and quality of education indicators released every year.

Acknowledgments

Many people are responsible for this book, and we must first recognize the support we have received from our families. Deven dedicates this book to Nina, who has gracefully put up with many evenings and weekends when Deven was holed up working on it. Mike dedicates this book to his wife, Michelle, and his sons, Sammy and Charlie.

The idea for this book is a product of both education and experience. Both authors have benefited greatly from the influence and ideas of colleagues and mentors who have expressed encouragement, support, and criticism. Mike would like to express thanks to Tom Snyder, Val Plisko, Marilyn Seastrom, and James P. Lynch as well as his former team at ESSI/AIR, including Mary Ann Fox, Grace Kena, Kevin Bianchi, Jana Kemp, and Katie Ferguson for their conversations, thoughts, and assistance. Others too numerous to mention at the National Center for Education Statistics and the American Institutes for Research have provided valuable insight to the workings we describe in this book. Deven would like to thank John Witte, Bob Haveman, Bobbi Wolfe, and Tom Kaplan, whose guidance, assistance, and support during his graduate studies have been invaluable. He would also like to thank his colleagues and faculty in the Interdisciplinary Training Program in Education Sciences and the Department of Political Science who have been the source of innumerable valuable conversations and suggestions. Finally, Deven would like to express gratitude to his former colleagues at the American Institutes for Research, especially his coauthor. This book would not have come together if not for Mike's ideas and efforts.

Finally, we would like to express our gratitude to our editors at Teachers College Press, Brian Ellerbeck and Lori Tate, and two anonymous reviewers who assessed the initial proposal for this book. Brian and Lori have provided wonderful guidance, suggestions, and enthusiasm for the project. We owe them for believing in our ideas and recognizing the value of this book.

CHAPTER 1

An Overview of Indicators

Statistical thinking will one day be as necessary for efficient citizenship as the ability to read and write.

—*H. G. Wells*

As we go about our daily lives we are regularly inundated with facts, figures, and statistics that describe all aspects of society. We consistently absorb nuggets of information that describe the status of the economy, government, health, crime, and leisure in America. Within minutes of opening the newspaper, turning on the television news, or browsing the Internet we will likely encounter statements similar to the following:

- Unemployment is rising.
- Crime is at record lows.
- The 85 and older population is expected to more than triple between 2008 and 2050.
- About 4 million adolescents smoke.
- An estimated 55 million children and teens were treated in emergency departments for unintentional injuries between 2001 and 2006.
- Civic engagement is declining in society.

Statistically based statements such as those presented above possess the virtues of concision and clarity. As such, they can provide clean, powerful, and convincing statements about a group or situation. The definitive nature of these statements does not invite dissension or debate about their accuracy. As a result, these simple statements can prove to be very compelling and often serve to ignite and drive policy debates.

The field of education is not any different from the domains referenced above. There is an abundance of information, from a wide variety of sources, that is used to monitor and report on the status and progress of our educational system. The groups disseminating this information range from the

1

federal government to teachers' unions to business groups that rely on the education system to produce skilled workers. Just as the sources of information vary widely, so do the goals of this information dissemination. Some groups, such as the government, may release this information in an effort to inform the public. Others, such as teachers' unions or business groups, may present data and information in hopes of influencing policy debates in a specific manner.

The popular media is often used as a vehicle for presenting and disseminating information on the education system. Major media outlets routinely provide extensive coverage of education indicators. A sampling of "findings" that have been reported by major media outlets within the past few years include:

- Students were victims of about 1.5 million crimes at school in 2005.
- Only 33% of fourth graders were proficient in reading.
- For the class of 2001, 72% of White students graduated from high school, but only half the Black, Hispanic, and American Indian children left with diplomas.
- About half of all new teachers leave the profession after just 5 years on the job.
- Only one-quarter of high school graduates who take college preparatory courses in high school are well prepared for college.

These statements are very direct, concrete, and convincing, and in some cases present dire situations for our children and the system in which they are educated. But upon what evidence are these statements based? Given the large emphasis that society places on using indicators as measures of performance and descriptions of status and change, the rarity with which we exercise any critical assessment of these measures is surprising. This is, in part, due to a lack of practical guidance to the audience on how to evaluate and assess indicator quality. Consumers are largely left on their own to navigate through this information and determine the legitimacy of the claims they encounter. Some may muddle through the voluminous technical reports that often accompany a substantive publication, but this documentation, if it is published at all, is often pedantic, arcane, and impossible to follow without an advanced degree in statistics or research methodology. As a result, it is not uncommon for individuals to develop an attitude that all numbers are of equal quality, are easy to manipulate, and offer little value to the issues at hand. A main purpose of this book is to dispel, or discourage the formation of, such attitudes. Numbers and indicators are not of equal quality, and the high-quality ones can be immensely valuable when considering important policy issues. The trick is to identify which indicators are of high quality and add value to policy debates.

Underlying individuals' distrust and pessimism toward indicators—and numbers more generally—is the fact that they often seem to be developed in mystical ways. The process through which these indicators are created is often less than transparent. How are high school dropout rates measured? What does proficiency in mathematics mean? What constitutes a violent crime at school? These seemingly straightforward issues can quickly become complicated once one considers the wide variety of ways these questions can be answered. While these issues certainly present difficulties, they can be overcome with careful consideration and evaluation.

We have all heard the quote often credited to Mark Twain:[1] "There are three kinds of lies: lies, damned lies, and statistics." Twain is certainly exaggerating when he refers to all statistics as gross distortions of the truth. In our opinion, statistics—or, more specifically, indicators—based on sound scientific procedures can be powerful tools for description, analysis, and monitoring change. Indicators of poor quality certainly distort and misguide decision making and policy. We believe that high-quality indicators are the overwhelming norm, but recognize that lies and distortions can be difficult for an uninformed audience to discern. This book takes the reader through the process and language associated with the production of education indicators in an effort to create a healthy skeptic and an informed citizen.

WHAT IS AN INDICATOR?

Identifying a clear and concise definition of an *indicator* seems like it should be a simple task. A quick review of past efforts to do so, however, reveals that it may not be as easy as it initially appears. Over the years scholars have defined an indicator in a number of different ways. These definitions are quite variable and, at times, even contradictory, disagreeing about aspects as fundamental as the basic purpose and contents of indicators (see Jaeger, 1978, and Land, 1983, for comprehensive reviews of the various definitions of indicators that scholars have proposed; more limited reviews can be found in Bauer, 1966; Bryk & Hermanson, 1993; Riley & Nuttall, 1994; and Oakes, 1986). Thankfully, cataloging the dozens of definitions of indicators and adjudicating among them is not central to the purpose of this book. Instead, we focus on identifying the features and characteristics of indicators that are commonly found in the existing definitions.

The first characteristic of an indicator that can be found in most definitions of the term is that they purport to describe the status of a specific condition or phenomenon. In the context of education, indicators may measure specific conditions such as student achievement, dropout rates, crime in schools, the condition of school buildings, literacy rates, or any number of other aspects of the educational landscape in America. While many indicators measure conditions that are quite specific and precise, they can also be developed to assess more general concepts, such as "academic success" or "college readiness." We discuss the distinctions between specific, or single, indicators and composite indicators at a later point in this chapter.

The second feature of indicators common to many definitions is their quantitative nature. Indicators are created from data and presented in the form of numbers and statistics. *Data* are observations that are generally collected in numerical form. For example, we might observe all high schools within a state and note the number and percentage of seniors within the schools who graduated at the end of the year. From these data we can derive *statistics,* a term that means "numerical facts." Statistics that are commonly used in the presentation of indicators include minimums, maximums, means, medians, and measures of dispersion, like the standard deviation. Continuing with the example of school-level data on the graduation of high school seniors, we could report the average percentage of seniors who graduated from high schools within the state. We could also report the percentage of seniors who graduated from the school with the lowest graduation rate (a minimum) and from the school with the highest graduation rate (a maximum). All of these numbers represent various statistics about graduating high school seniors. In effect, statistics take observations, or data, and organize the information in terms of quantitative properties.

Combining these two commonly identified features of indicators provides us with a solid idea of the primary purpose and goals of indicators. Specifically, indicators combine statistics with purpose, meaning, and context to provide useful information about a condition or phenomenon of interest.

The discussion to this point may lead readers to wonder about the difference between a statistic and an indicator. Hopefully, we have made clear that indicators are generally composed of statistics, but that not all statistics are indicators. Jeannie Oakes (1986) perhaps provides the clearest description of the distinction between indicators and statistics when she writes: "For a statistic to be an indicator, it must have a standard against which it can be judged. Indicators must meet certain substantive and technical standards that define the kind of information they should measure" (p. vii). In other words, statistics need context, purpose, and meaning if they are going to be considered an indicator.

One final feature that can be found in a number of definitions of indicators is the existence of a temporal component. That is, some definitions require an indicator not only to monitor the status of a condition or phenomenon at a certain point in time but also to have the ability to examine the change in the condition over time. Taking a concrete example, the 2009 Condition of Education (Planty et al., 2009) tells us that 49.3 million students were enrolled in K–12 public schools in the United States in 2006. This information is interesting and informative by itself, but the information gains additional value when we compare it to enrollment in prior years and enrollment projections for future years. Indeed, we see that 10 years earlier, in 1996, 45.6 million students were enrolled in K–12 public schools in the United States and 10 years in the future, in 2016, the Department of Education projects 52.9 million students to be enrolled in K–12. By observing enrollment trends over time, we can gain an understanding of the implications that enrollment trends will have on the education system. For example, by looking at enrollment trends and projections over time, we can see that the education system will likely need to hire additional teachers and build more school buildings. Such conclusions could not be reached by examining enrollment at a single point in time.

By describing the characteristics of indicators, we are not intentionally avoiding explicitly defining the term. However, with the wealth of existing definitions, we do not think it would be useful to add yet another to the pool. Instead, we point readers toward two definitions that we believe capture the essence of an indicator in a clear and concise manner. The first of these definitions was put forth by R. Jaeger (1978) and encapsulates many of the qualities of an indicator that other definitions identify. He felt that an indicator could best be described through a two-part definition, and states that an indicator (1) "represents the aggregate status or change in status of any group of persons, objects, institutions, or elements under study, and (2) is essential to a report of status or change of status of the entities under study or to an understanding of the condition of the entities under study" (p. 285). The second definition is broader and was developed in the context of education indicators. Oakes (1986), in probably the most recognized piece on education indicators written, provides the following definition: "An educational indicator is a statistic that tells something about the performance or health of the education system" (p. vii). While these definitions are quite different stylistically, they capture the main goal and purpose of an indicator, and provide a good starting point for thinking about indicators.

TYPES OF INDICATORS

All indicators can be classified as either a single or composite statistic (Oakes, 1986). A *single statistic* is a measure of one specific aspect of the education system. The mean standardized test score in a school, the median teacher salary in a school district, the number of students enrolled in public schools in a state, and the number of states with charter school laws are just a few examples of single statistics. While single statistics are often conceptually straightforward and not overly complex, they can provide a wealth of useful and descriptive information about the education system. Just as single statistics like the temperature, humidity, wind speed, and dew point provide a clear and informative description about the weather, the status of our nation's education system can be described by single-statistic indicators. Standardized test scores, dropout statistics, and teacher salaries represent a few of the most common single statistics that are used to describe the status of the education system.

Whereas single statistics provide information about one aspect of the education system, composite statistics represent a relationship between two or more concepts or aspects of the education system. Composite indicators are created by combining multiple single statistics into one measure. Perhaps the most common and straightforward example of a composite indicator is the student-teacher ratio, which represents a relationship between enrollment and the number of teachers in a classroom, school, district, or state. Unlike the stock market's Dow Jones Industrial Average, education does not have a single composite indicator defining educational success or status (Guthrie, 1993; Riley & Nuttall, 1994).

Composite indicators are often used to summarize multiple dimensions of a concept into a single measure. For example, SAT scores and high school coursework can be combined to create a measure of college readiness. With the No Child Left Behind Act of 2001 (NCLB, 2002), two composite indicators—adequate yearly progress and highly qualified teachers—have emerged as quite prominent features of the American educational landscape. *Adequate yearly progress* (AYP) is a composite indicator that combines standardized test scores with attendance records to measure the academic success of each school throughout the country. To be considered as making adequate yearly progress, schools and districts must exhibit satisfactory test scores and attendance records for each of a wide variety of demographic subgroups (NCLB, 2002, Sec. 1111).

The No Child Left Behind Act of 2001 also included provisions regarding the presence of highly qualified teachers, a measure that is a clear example of a composite indicator. Under the NCLB legislation, teachers are considered to be highly qualified if they (1) hold a bachelor's degree; (2) possess full state certification and licensing; and (3) demonstrate competency in their subject area through their college major/coursework or a state-developed test. School districts and states are required to report the percentage of students taught by highly qualified teachers, with particular emphasis on the proportion of minority and disadvantaged students taught by highly qualified teachers. The emphasis placed on adequate yearly progress and highly qualified teachers in the current policy environment illustrates the utility and importance of composite education indicators (NCLB, 2002, Sec. 9101).

Composite indicators are generally more conceptually complex than single statistics, but they are often preferable to attempting to draw conclusions from comparing and assessing multiple single statistics. Consuming a single, prefabricated measure of college readiness is easier than examining SAT scores and then moving on to assess high school coursework in order to reach a conclusion on the topic of college readiness. While composite indicators possess the twin virtues of simplicity and clarity, they can also lead to oversimplification of complex problems and misleading interpretation of important issues.

PURPOSES OF INDICATORS

There are three primary purposes of most indicators. First, they can be used to report on the status of a particular topic or policy area in the education system. Second, they can be used to monitor change over time for a particular topic or policy area within the education system. Third, they can be used to project future patterns. From these uses, one can describe the health or condition of our educational system, inform policy decisions, or hold actors (students, teachers, schools, districts, or even states) accountable. For example, schools can be held accountable for their students' academic performance either through measures of status (all students meeting a specific proficiency level) or by change (students continue to make progress on standardized test scores) (Murnane, 1987; Zvoch & Stevens, 2008).

Of their three primary purposes, indicators are most often used to report on the status of a group. The number of students who take algebra, the percentage of minorities who drop out of high school, and the percentage of students who use loans to finance their postsecondary education are all examples of reports on the status of a group. Indicators that report on the status of a group are ubiquitous and are likely encountered by many people on a near-daily basis.

Monitoring status indicators over time can describe change. Indicators can be monitored over both short and long periods of time. For example, the Department of Education routinely issues reports that present results from the National Assessment of Educational Progress stretching back to the 1960s, which is clearly a long period of time over which progress has been monitored. Other reports from the Department of Education, however, present achievement results dating back only to the 1990s. Indicators that stretch over short- or long-term time periods can describe patterns or be used to monitor or evaluate policy decisions. Further, disaggregating larger trends by select demographics (such as race, gender, or socioeconomic status) can reveal important differences in the timing, magnitude, and duration of specific group trends.

Projecting future patterns is another valuable feature of indicators (e.g., see NCES, 2008). Placed in the context of what is already known, projections can serve to provide guidance on future trends, identify challenges, and establish goals. For example, changes in the size and characteristics of student enrollments or potential teacher shortages can have direct impacts on institutional budgets and decision making by educators and administrators.

In addition to their three main purposes described above, indicators also have a number of more strategic uses. Status indicators are often used in formula allocations for government programs (Melnick, 2002). For example, in an effort to assist schools with the highest student concentrations of poverty, the federal government's Title I legislation allows states to distribute funds to school districts on the basis of an indicator, specifically the number and proportion of students eligible for free and reduced-price lunch.

Performance indicators are a special and important type of status indicator that have gained considerable attention in education (e.g., Murnane, 1987; Zvoch & Stevens, 2008). *Performance indicators* are used to evaluate student progress, and evaluate teachers and schools. Two indicators discussed in the previous section—adequate yearly progress and highly qualified teachers—serve as prime examples of performance indicators. They accomplish the traditional purpose of painting a descriptive portrait about one or more aspects of the education system, but they are also used to levy sanctions and provide rewards to schools, districts, and states. For example, schools or districts that perform poorly on the adequate yearly progress indicator are subject to a variety of sanctions, ranging from the requirement to provide supplementary educational services (i.e., after-school tutoring) to a complete overhaul of the school or district leadership.

Indicators also serve to inform research. Many of the important research questions in education came to light because of indicators. For example, research on the causes of the Black–White achievement gap was undertaken after indicators showed the existence of a large discrepancy in achievement between racial groups. Similarly, the recent emphasis on identifying methods for controlling college costs is based on the observation that college costs have been rising rapidly over time, an observation that was made possible by the existence of indicators that monitor change over time on this topic. Current research often focuses on sophisticated research design and modeling techniques, but it is important to remember that a fundamental characteristic of good research involves describing the issue and stating the research question. Observation is clearly a critical first step to the research process, and indicators play an important role in this step.

HISTORY OF EDUCATION INDICATORS

Indicators have long been used to describe the state of the economy and labor market, but their influence on other aspects of society is a more recent phenomenon. Specifically, it was during the 1960s that *Social Indicators*, the seminal work by Raymond Bauer (1966), began to foster a reliance on and interest in the use of indicators. Over the next few decades they would be used to describe all aspects of the human condition, including education (Jaeger, 1978; Land, 1983). In education a variety of organizations at the national, state, and local levels have contributed to the collection and dissemination of information on the status of education in America.

National and International Indicator Efforts

At the national level, information on the status of education has been collected for over 100 years. A detailed collection of historical statistics and indicators is presented in the report *120 Years of American Education: A Statistical Portrait* (Snyder, 1993). This report describes the evolution of what began as the Center for Education and is now referred to as the U.S. Department of Education, and more specifically, the National Center for Education Statistics (NCES):

> In 1867, the Congress of the United States passed legislation providing "That there shall be established at the City of Washington, a department of education, for the purpose of collecting such statistics and facts as shall show the condition and progress of education in the several States and Territories, and of diffusing such information respecting the organization and management of schools and school systems, and methods of teaching, as shall aid the people of the United States in the establishment and maintenance of efficient school systems, and otherwise promote the cause of education throughout the country." (p. 1)

The value and purpose of statistics at the federal level have experienced many ebbs and flows over the last 140 years, and the statistics center has faced many challenges to properly fulfill its mandate to "collect" and "diffuse" statistics. Throughout most of the early years, due to limitations in technology, data collection procedures, resources, and cooperation, national statistics were of varying quality. The staff gradually grew from 16 in 1948 to 76 in 1957 to a staff of 130 in 2008. Currently, the NCES serves as the centerpiece for monitoring the health and progress of our nation's educational system from early childhood through adulthood. The NCES collects, analyzes, and reports education statistics in the United States. Its publications, like *The Condition of Education* (Planty et al., 2008, 2009), serve as valuable resources for educators, administrators, journalists, and policy makers. The information contained in these publications is derived from administrative records and data collected through large-scale, standardized surveys and assessments. These collections include information on the participation and enrollment in schooling, academic performance, persistence and attainment, and contextual indicators about schooling environment, conditions, faculty, and finances.

A primary focus for the Center involved the valid assessment of academic performance. In 1969 the Center launched the National Assessment of Educational Progress (NAEP) to monitor student achievement over time. Often referred to as the "Nation's Report Card," the program is responsible for assessing a nationally representative sample of U.S. 4th, 8th, and 12th graders across multiple subject areas.

There are many organizations outside of government that disseminate indicators with a national focus. Some are tailored toward a specific sector. For example, the American Association of Community Colleges (AACC) routinely produces statistics and trends about community college students, faculty, and institutions (e.g., see AACC, 2010). Other organizations focus on a particular issue. For example, the National Science Foundation (NSF, n.d.) has developed an indicator system for science and engineering capturing education, workforce, international, and social indicators. Internationally, the Organization for Economic Co-operation and Development (OECD) publishes a series of indicators in the annual publication *Education at a Glance 2008: OECD Indicators* (OECD, 2008). OECD indicators provide timely, cross-country comparisons on a number of indicators representing participation in education, costs, performance, context of education, and outcomes of education.

State and Local Indicator Efforts

The use and reports of indicators is hardly restricted to federal government institutions. Schools, school districts, and state education agencies collect and diffuse information on a wide variety of educational topics. They assess students and set performance goals, create budgets, record attendance, monitor school discipline and violence, count graduates, create academic transcripts, and harbor a tremendous amount of information on teachers and other staff. State programs on education indicators often produce state profiles, accountability systems, and report cards on progress (Selden, 1994). The increased pressure in recent years to demand more accountability from our schools and educators has resulted in an explosion of such indicators. States, districts, and schools collect and disseminate statistics for the purpose of description, performance measurement, management, and compliance with federal and state regulations. Outside of government, the Council of Chief State School Officers (CCSSO) is an organization intimately involved in monitoring the progress of state policies in education. The CCSSO has developed a comprehensive set of state-level education indicators (Blank, 1993; CCSSO, n.d.). Regardless of the governmental agency or private organization that generates an indicator, the most critical aspect of collecting and administering information is to ensure high-quality information. Indicators constructed of poor quality can only serve to distort or misinform policy and our understanding of education.

QUALITIES OF A GOOD INDICATOR

Providing the reader with an understanding and general framework for understanding and evaluating indicators is the primary goal of this book. The first step in accomplishing this goal involves describing the characteristics of a high-quality indicator. In short, good indicators are

- Valid
- Reliable
- Timely
- Transparent
- Relevant
- Purposeful

Of all these characteristics, validity is the most central concept. Simply put, the concept of *validity* refers to whether you are actually measuring what you intend to measure (Adcock & Collier, 2001; Bollen, 1989; King, Keohane, & Verba, 1994; Pedhazur & Schmelkin, 1991). Cook and Campbell (1979) define it as the "best available approximation to the truth or falsity of a given proposition" (p. 37). Researchers have identified many types of validity, and the main concern in this book is measurement validity. *Measurement validity* is "specifically concerned with whether operationalization and the scoring of cases adequately reflect the concept the researcher seeks to measure" (Adcock & Collier, 2001). For example, when we say 50% of fourth graders are proficient in mathematics, how certain are we that each element of this statement is accurate? That is, are we sure we included only fourth graders and a representative group of fourth graders, did we do an adequate job testing what we call "mathematics," and do we have an accepted working definition for "proficient"? How we operationalize these concepts is directly related to indicator quality. Any deviation from these elements will introduce error.

Reliability is the second feature of a high-quality indicator. *Reliability* is the extent to which a measure yields consistent estimates. It refers to the degree of variance in an estimate when it is measured the same way under the same condition with the same subjects. Returning to our mathematics assessment example, will students perform the "same" if they are given the test twice? Or do they exhibit wildly different scores? If a student scores at the advanced level one day and then at the below-basic level the next, the reliability of such an assessment is low. A high degree of reliability gives us a measure of confidence that the indicator is of good quality. For many large-scale surveys, reliability is linked to the sample size. If only a small number of sample members respond to a question, the estimate will have a low level of reliability or precision. For example, in large national surveys estimates for small minority populations (Asians, American Indians) tend to be unreliable since only a small number of respondents are selected to participate in the survey. To compensate for this imprecision, many surveys will oversample these groups of interest. Other factors that affect reliability include how questions are constructed, how varied the respondent answers are to questions, and variation in the conditions in how the survey is administered or information is collected. It is important to note that a reliable estimate is not necessarily a valid one. It is possible to consistently produce an estimate that does not reflect the concept that you are trying to measure.

Often people refer to an estimate as either being either reliable or unreliable, and valid or invalid. These dichotomies are of limited use since indicators are never completely reliable or valid. Instead, the concepts of reliability and validity can best be conceived as lying along continuums. There are degrees of reliability and validity. Figure 1.1 represents a graphical depiction of the range through which the quality indicators may fall. Generally speaking, indicators that have high levels of validity and reliability are considered quality indicators (depicted as Section A). As we move down either axis, the quality of an indicator suffers. Section B relates to indicators with a high validity, but suspect reliability, with Section C capturing indicators with high reliability but of lower validity. Section D represents indicators of limited quality—low reliability and validity. However, depending on an indicator's purpose and use, having a moderate degree of reliability and/or validity may serve a purpose just fine.

In addition to being valid and reliable, high-quality indicators are timely. Timeliness has three specific dimensions. The first dimension refers to the

Figure 1.1. Degrees of reliability and validity

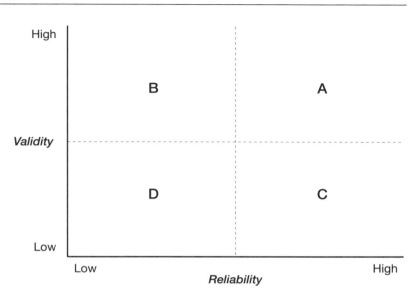

length of time required to collect the data, analyze it, and make the results available to the public. It is preferable to make results available as soon as possible after the collection of data. The second dimension of timeliness is the frequency with which data on a specific topic are collected. If we are interested in understanding student academic progress, a yearly assessment may be most desirable. However, if we are interested in teacher demographics, then we might only need to collect information every 2 or 3 years, since these characteristics do not vary greatly from year to year. The third dimension of timeliness refers to the specific timing of a measurement. Consider the assessment of student math skills. Were these skills assessed in early spring when they were only a little more than halfway through the school year? Or was it at the beginning of the school year after 3 months of summer break? Clearly, the timing of the assessment could have an influence on the results. Each dimension of timeliness we identify above has critical implications for understanding the value of indicators.

To be of high quality, indicators should be transparent to their intended audience. By transparency, we mean that the methods used to develop the indicator, collect and analyze the data, and report the results should be clear to the audience. Technical reports or the supporting documentation of an indicator can serve to illustrate the level of transparency of an indicator. Indicators must also be relevant to meet the needs of the intended audience.

Relevance is directly connected with the factors described above; users will find less value in indicators that are not timely, lack validity, are unreliable, or do not reflect current policy.

Indicators that are created for a specific purpose will often be of better quality and easier to understand. The higher level of quality in indicators with a specific purpose can be attributed to the fact that issues concerning data quality can be noted and resolved when the purpose of the indicator is defined prior to the creation and data collection phases. Problems with indicators tend to surface when indicators are created from data that were collected for a wholly different purpose. For example, schools and districts often collect data in order to comply with state or federal reporting requirements. Because they have already been collected, these data are often subsequently used to create indicators for concepts that are only tangentially connected to the original purpose for which the data were collected. Such practices have the potential to result in indicators of lesser quality.

A FRAMEWORK FOR UNDERSTANDING INDICATOR QUALITY

As we hinted at above, indicators cannot be judged on a dichotomous scale. They are not either high-quality or low-quality. Rather, they must be judged on a continuum. Since indicator quality is determined largely through the management of indicator construction, the framework presented here describes how the quality of an indicator is affected at each step during creation.

In order to evaluate the overall quality of an indicator, it is important to understand the error structure of the indicator. The *error structure* is an estimate of indicator quality. That is, it is the difference between the "true" answer and what you actually collect, analyze, and report. Researchers generally deal with two main types of error: sampling and nonsampling error. *Sampling error* occurs because we don't collect information from everyone in the population. In many cases, especially with large-scale national surveys, it is not efficient, practical, or economical to survey everyone in the population. Imagine trying to collect standardized test scores and information about student behaviors from every high school senior in the United States at the same time. With a graduating class of around 3 million students each year the logistics would be very expensive and time-consuming, basically impractical. When these concerns are coupled with the fact that very precise estimates can be produced with only a sample of the population, it becomes very clear that attempting to collect information from the entire population is a very poor option. The error associated with taking a sample is relatively easy to know in advance. Researchers can determine the level of precision in the planning stages of their design. Where sample sizes are very small or when responses are highly varied, sampling error tends to be larger. In other words, the estimates are less precise.

The other general error is referred to as nonsampling or measurement error. Measurement error includes everything but sampling error and is related to a number of factors. Whom did you ask and who responded to the request for information? How were the questions constructed? How were the observations collected (paper-and-pencil format, telephone, or computer)? Were some questions not answered? What was the source of information (student, teacher, principal)? When did we collect the data (beginning, during, or at the end of the school year)? How was the data collected and analyzed? How was it presented? Each of these issues has the potential to introduce nonsampling error. Over time, several approaches have been developed to measure the potential amount of nonsampling error. Measures such as these are often referred to as *paradata* and can be thought of as descriptions about the data and the collection process (Couper & Lyberg, 2005). Paradata include measures such as the unit response rate, item or question response rate, the coverage rate, and measures of bias that may be induced by individuals failing to respond to surveys or specific items within a survey. By generating quantitative information about the data that have been collected, we are in effect creating indicators that can be used to inform us about the quality of the data. Additional aspects of paradata include descriptions and observations about respondents, the interviewers used to collect the data, and specific interviewing techniques. Such information provides individuals with a window into how the details of data collection process could affect the quality of the data, both positively and negatively.

The process of indicator creation involves five general steps: conceptualization, operationalization, analysis, interpretation, and presentation. Each of these steps are discussed in detail in the subsequent chapters, but a brief introduction is useful now. *Conceptualization* is the process of "formulating a systemized concept through reasoning about the background concepts, in light of the research goals" (Adcock and Collier, 2001). It involves generating an explicit definition of the concept that one is trying to measure. Often the definition is a product of expert consensus, but error may be introduced when the definition does not include all aspects of the concept.

Operationalization is the process of defining and translating the conceptual definition into a concrete measure. Measurement involves data collection, and data collection involves all of the issues and decisions as to how to collect the measure. From who or where do we get the information? How do we get this information from the source? When do we collect this information? These are only a few general questions involved in the operationalization process. From a practical standpoint, the researcher must decide whether a student, teacher, principal, parent, or administrative record is the best source for gathering information about a specific topic. This operation is guided by the conceptual definition, but also constrained by considerations of costs, timing, and resource availability, among others. Common sources of error introduced at this stage are related to respondent bias, respondent misinterpreting the question, variation in the presentation of the questions by how information is collected, and many others.

The data used to produce an indicator can be collected from samples or from the entire population in a particular group, referred to as a *universe*. Of course, for cases where data are collected from all individuals in the population, often referred to as *universe data,* there is no sampling error. For example, many states have information about all of their students or staff. As a result, they are not concerned with sampling error. Samples present additional problems with collection, analysis, and presentation because it is necessary to project responses from a subset of individuals to the entire population. Making these projections has the potential to introduce error.

Regardless of whether data will be collected from a sample or from the entire population, analysts must decide upon the method through which they will collect the data that will be used to create an indicator. That is, they must identify the source of information. There are several potential sources of information, but one of the most common involves collecting data directly from the individuals that an indicator is designed to describe. For example, we can collect information about individual students' academic achievement by administering a mathematics assessment. We can learn about their victimization history by asking them how many times they were assaulted. We can gain information about their educational attainment by inquiring whether they graduated from high school with a regular or honors diploma. In cases such as these, error can be introduced if individuals are not the most appropriate or accurate source of information. For example, asking high school students about their course grades tend to result in an upward bias; students inflate their grades when compared to their official transcripts.

Another option is to rely on administrative data or official records. Most facets of education and educational organizations are measured and recorded in detail: budgets, teacher characteristics, benefits and salaries, transportation, assessments, and a litany of other resources. Official records are kept from students' entry to preschool programs and extend through their postsecondary careers and job training activities, capturing a range of information that includes attendance patterns, academic performance, behavioral problems and extracurricular activities. While administrative data have several advantages, they can also present challenges to data quality in several ways. The primary errors related to administrative records include a

lack of standardization across units and coverage error. The practice of recording and classifying events often varies between schools and even within
schools. Knowing that a student in one school received an A in calculus and
a student in a different school received a B may not tell you very much about
their individual mathematics abilities without some knowledge of course
curriculum and academic demands. Further, not all students take calculus,
which can lead to coverage error. It may that there are significant differences
between the types of students enrolled in these courses that are heavily dependent on school practices.

Negotiating between these two general data collection approaches is not
an easy task. Each will have the possibility of introducing error. Trade-offs
between collection time, costs, information availability, and quality must be
balanced within a given purpose for obtaining the information in the first
place.

Next, we collectively group the final three steps of indicator creation under the general umbrella of *dissemination.* This is the process of taking the
information collected through the data collection process, producing statistics and indicators, and presenting these estimates in tables, charts, and text
to a targeted audience. It involves *analysis, interpretation,* and data *presentation.* Most often indicators are presented as descriptive statistics; counts,
percentages, rates, and proportions are common metrics. These metrics are
often shown in graphical form or tables. The development and presentation
of indicators can have serious implications in terms of how they are interpreted and understood (Best, 2001; Huff, 1954).

As we work through each step, the reader will gain an understanding
of what type of error is associated with each decision. This leads to an understanding of the estimate's error structure. After each step we develop an
estimate of how far away the indicator is from the "truth" and decide if the
error is acceptable given the purpose.

LIMITATIONS AND DISTORTIONS

The use of indicators is a double-edged sword. Indicators can serve as a
valuable tool to describe status and trends over time and provide critical information to inform policy decisions. However, as Donald Campbell (1976)
warned: "The more any quantitative social indicator is used for social decision making, the more subject it will be to corruption pressures and the
more apt it will be to distort and corrupt the social processes it is intended
to monitor" (p. 49).

Huff's (1954) work presents the classic examples of the limitations and
distortions of statistics and indicators. Recent work by scholars has continued to document specific instances and examples in sociology (Best, 2001,

2004) and more specifically education (Bracey, 2004). Further, there can also be an overreliance on indicators and a perception that if you can measure something, you can solve the problem. Hess (2008) describes three situations in which data can lead to negative consequences: using data regardless of quality, overgeneralizing findings, and placing an overemphasis on outcome indicators without knowledge of inputs or context.

ORGANIZATION OF THE BOOK

H.G. Wells understood the importance of quantitative literacy when he stated, "Statistical thinking will one day be as necessary for efficient citizenship as the ability to read and write."[2] Others such as Crossen (1994) evaluated the current state of statistical literacy in her groundbreaking book *Tainted Truth,* stating:

> American schools, which have largely ignored the explosion of quantitative information in daily life, can and should teach people how to tell whether particular sets of numbers are believable. Learning information skills should be as important to high school and college as a working knowledge of literature, science, economics or communications. (p. 227)

The purpose of this book is a modest one. It is to provide users with a framework and tools for understanding and evaluating the quality and value of education indicators. We provide readers with an overview of how indicators are generated and used in education. The reader is presented with the process of conceptualization, measurement, and dissemination. The seemingly straightforward process is, in actuality, rather complex, but it is our hope that this complexity becomes transparent and the reader gains an appreciation for the value and limitations associated with construction of education indicators.

Chapter 2, "Measurement," describes the construction of an indicator from a concept to a published estimate for the consumer. Establishing a working taxonomy that is reliable and valid is critical. The key issue addressed in this section is measurement validity—does the indicator adequately reflect the concept the researcher seeks to measure?

Chapter 3, "Sources of Information and Error," provides a framework for understanding an indicator's general error structure by outlining the sources of information and identifying common types of errors associated with these sources. Data are collected from everyone in a particular group or from samples of the entire population, which involves projecting responses from a subset to the entire population. Information can be collected from individuals themselves or from administrative data, including student transcripts, principal enrollment counts, or official reports of discipline, such as student suspensions.

Chapter 4, "Statistics and Data Presentation," describes basic statistical concepts and estimates used in the presentation and interpretation of education indicators. The first section of this chapter includes a discussion of basic concepts including common metrics (percents, counts, percentiles), measures of central tendency (mean, modes, median), measures of dispersion (standard deviation, range), change scores, and trend analysis. Next is a presentation on standard errors associated with samples, statistical significance testing, substantive significance, power, and effect sizes. Special attention is given to achievement test scores and proficiency scores and rankings. Attention will be given to the use of weights and sample design variables. The third section describes how data are presented in tables and charts, outlining the important elements to consider during this process, including which type of graph should be used, the choice of scales, presenting time series data, and so on. We devote a significant amount of space to address the topic of student assessments and the creation of performance indicators.

Chapter 5, "The Misuse of Statistical Indicators," describes how indicators, when created with all good intentions, can be easily misused. Intentional or not, statistics are often misinterpreted, misunderstood, distorted, or just plain wrong. Misuse of indicators can have serious consequences. We provide a series of questions and examples of some common errors in presenting data, along with appropriate fixes.

CHAPTER 2

Measurement

I believe that the most serious and important problems that require our immediate and concerted attention are those of conceptualization and measurement, which have far too long been neglected. In fact they are so complex, and their implications for analysis so serious, that I believe that a really coordinated effort in this direction is absolutely essential.

—H. M. Blalock, Jr.

In his 1979 presidential address to the American Sociological Association, H. M. Blalock, Jr. emphasized the problems and difficulties associated with the conceptualization and measurement of constructs and ideas in empirical research (Blalock, 1979). He highlighted how the issues of conceptualization and measurement can affect the execution of research, and noted that the issues can even shape the substantive conclusions that emerge from such research. Even though Blalock's address was delivered over 30 years ago, the problems and issues he identified are no less relevant today. These issues remain germane to all sorts of research and policy work, especially including the creation of indicators. Indeed, the topics of conceptualization and measurement lie at the very heart of indicator creation, and researchers and policy analysts must devote careful consideration to these topics when developing an indicator.

The process of indicator creation begins with the development and clear presentation of the concept that the researcher is attempting to describe. This seems like it should be a relatively simple task, but there are almost always a variety of complexities that must be addressed to provide a clear description of a concept. For example, suppose that an indicator purports to describe dropout rates, a concept that is seemingly quite straightforward. However, there are many subtle intricacies that must be addressed before the concept of a dropout is entirely clear: Does a student who obtained a GED in place of a regular diploma count as a dropout? If a student drops in and out of school throughout the school year, what date or length of time should determine when the student should be counted as a dropout? Thus, providing a comprehensive and lucid description of the concept is not as simple as it may initially seem. This chapter will describe effective methods of conceptualization and demonstrate the importance of doing so.

In addition to presenting a clear description of the concept underlying the indicator, another important step in indicator creation involves identifying and developing a method of measuring that concept. Conceptual definitions must be developed into *concrete items,* ones that can be measured. The measure must be both reliable and valid, two criteria that we touched on in the previous chapter and will describe in greater detail at a later point in this chapter. Going back to the dropout example discussed above, there are a variety of potential ways to measure the number of dropouts. For example, a researcher could survey a nationally representative sample of individuals aged 16–19 and ask them whether they had dropped out of school. Alternatively, the researcher could use a unique identifier and track student annual enrollment and mobility patterns. Both of these measures could potentially be used to gauge the number of dropouts, but as we explore later, they will likely perform quite differently on the criteria of reliability and validity. Thus, performing the tasks of conceptualization and measurement in an ad hoc or disorganized manner can lead to an unreliable or invalid indicator, which has the potential to severely undermine the indicator's utility.

While measurement represents an important, if not the most important, aspect of indicator creation, it is far from the only step involved. Indeed, the process of indicator creation is a demanding, multistep process that usually begins with a nascent concept and ends with a published estimate for the consumer, with many steps in between. Many of these steps take place concurrently, and it can be difficult to cleanly separate the stages of indicator creation. However, this chapter will provide a thorough description of the measurement process, with discrete examples. We begin by discussing concept formation and the emergence of indicators from the perception of a problem.

ORIGINS OF INDICATORS

In Chapter 1, we stated that indicators are often used to report on the status of a group or measure a specific concept or phenomenon in the educational arena. As a result, it is not surprising that indicators arise in response to a perceived problem in the educational arena. The origination of the indicator creation process often takes place when educators, politicians, the general public, or some other stakeholder perceives a specific problem in the nation's education system. To get an accurate sense of the magnitude of the problem they perceive, policy makers or researchers work to develop indicators that provide a direct and accurate measurement of the phenomenon. These indicators then serve to shape the perception of the problem.

One recent topic that has embodied this process is that of teacher quality. In the late 1990s concerns began to emerge over the quality and training of the nation's teaching force (see Darling-Hammond, 2000). These concerns quickly gained steam within the education policy community, and policy analysts had soon developed indicators measuring the qualifications of the teaching force (McMillen-Seastrom, Gruber, Henke, McGrath, & Cohen, 2002). Policy makers even codified a definition of *highly qualified teacher* into federal legislation. According to the No Child Left Behind Act of 2001, teachers must: (1) possess a bachelor's degree, (2) possess full state certification or licensure, and (3) prove that they know each subject they teach (NCLB, 2002, Sec. 9101).

In addition to specifying a definition of a highly qualified teacher, No Child Left Behind also requires school districts to produce an indicator on the topic. Specifically, for each of several demographic subgroups, it requires districts to publish the proportion of students taught by highly qualified teachers. The indicator helps policy makers monitor the qualifications and allocation of the nation's teaching force. This scenario presents a clear case where an indicator emerged in response to a perceived problem or concept of interest. Figure 2.1 illustrates how an indicator can emerge to promote a better understanding of the problem and, ultimately, to inform policy. The figure also shows how the relationship is cyclical, with policy makers continually using indicators to monitor the status of a problem, updating their understanding of the problem, and deciding whether to take policy action.

MOVING FROM ORIGINATION
TO CONCEPTUALIZATION TO OBSERVATION

After it has been determined that a concept is important and an indicator should be developed to gauge the status of a perceived problem in the education system, the next step in the indicator creation process involves specifying and clarifying the precise concept that the indicator will be designed to measure. This process is broadly referred by several terms, including conceptualization, measurement, and operationalization. The process can be parsed into three general steps: conceptual definition, operational definition, and concrete measurement or observation (Babbie, 2005). Here we take an abstract concept and attempt to generate concrete measures of that concept. For example, student academic achievement can be measured by grade point average or SAT scores. These are certainly not the only measures we can use. The process

Figure 2.1. Indicator origination and development process

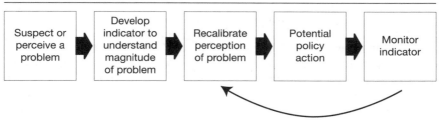

can be difficult and subject to considerable debate, but it is always important. The manner in which an indicator is conceptualized plays a large role in determining its quality and value.

Conceptual Definition

Several significant decisions must be made throughout the conceptualization process. First and foremost is the presentation of a conceptual definition. This definition describes, in the abstract, the qualities and concepts that the indicator will purport to describe. To draw on the example presented in the previous section, indicators have been developed that are conceptually defined as measuring the qualifications of the teaching force. Additional examples of conceptual definitions of indicators are the following:

- Student readiness for college
- Persistently dangerous schools
- Mathematics and science course taking
- Mathematics proficiency
- Adequacy of school financial resources
- Student engagement
- Student-teacher ratios
- Extent of out-of-field teaching

Some conceptual definitions are broad and abstract—such as student readiness for college—while others are narrower and more tractable, like student-teacher ratios. The challenges of measurement are not limited to these more complex concepts. Defining seemingly simple characteristics such as student race, ethnicity, disability status, and poverty have obvious policy implications. Regardless of their breadth, conceptual definitions are useful for stating the purpose of an indicator and focusing its attention on a specific topic.

Operational Definition

While presenting a conceptual definition for an indicator is important, it is only the first step in the process of conceptualization. Such definitions identify the phenomenon that will be described, but they are silent on how the concept will be concretely defined. The second stage of conceptualization involves moving beyond a broad conceptual definition. In this stage, decisions must be made regarding the operationalization of the concept. Put another way, the tasks at the second stage of conceptualization move to developing a concrete, operational (or working) definition for the indicator and identifying the precise measures that will be used to represent the concept described in the conceptual definition. This step is among the most difficult in the indicator creation process. It is often quite difficult to move from an abstract concept to a concrete, operational definition.

Consider our running example where an indicator was conceptually defined to measure the qualifications of the teaching force. At the second stage of conceptualization, it is necessary to concretely determine how teacher qualifications will be operationally defined. Such a task is not easy; there are literally dozens of ways that teacher qualifications could plausibly be defined. To list a few, qualifications could be defined by the academic degrees held by teachers, the number of years of experience that teachers have, the attainment of certain teacher certifications, their students' academic performance on standardized tests, or ratings made by principals or district superintendents.

Let's take another example. Suppose we are interested in developing an indicator that measures high school mathematics course taking, a seemingly straightforward concept. However, coming up with an operational definition of mathematics course taking is not as simple as it may seem. It is not obvious which courses should be classified as mathematics courses and which should not. For example, should computer programming be considered a math course? These courses imbue an understanding of logical statements that are fundamental to many aspects of mathematics, but it is not clear that these classes should be classified as mathematics courses. What about consumer economics courses? They often cover topics such as interest rates and compound interest, which undeniably rely on principles of mathematics. However, the purpose of these courses is to prepare individuals to make intelligent personal economic decisions, not develop fundamental mathematics skills. Considerations such as these can complicate the development of an operational definition.

In a third example, consider an indicator that was developed to measure expenditures on student instruction. Indeed, many states have enacted legislation that requires a certain proportion of school district budgets to be spent on student instruction. Developing an operational definition of student instruction expenditures is not fully straightforward. Such a definition would likely include expenditures on items such as textbooks and teacher salaries, but what about expenditures on extracurricular activities such as science clubs or debate teams? The line between instructional and noninstructional expenditures is certainly blurry, and the difficulties associated with moving from an abstract, conceptual definition to a concrete, operational definition are again clear.

Ultimately, the development of operational definitions necessitates a reliance on some sort of classification scheme or taxonomy. *Taxonomies* are a way to organize information into discrete categories or classifications that are substantively different from one another. These categories can often be used as the basis for the development of an operational definition. To provide a concrete example, consider the example presented above regarding the construction of an operational definition of expenditures on student instruction. In this case, the creator of the indicator could look to the Common Core of Data, a database maintained by the National Center for Education Statistics, for a taxonomy of expenditures, particularly expenditures on student instruction. Specifically, the Common Core of Data identifies eight categories of instructional expenditures, including teacher salaries, teacher benefits, supplies, textbooks, and several others. Any or all of these categories could be included in the development of an operational definition of instructional expenditures. Similarly, the development of an operational definition for mathematics course taking could draw on any number of taxonomies that classify mathematics courses, such as the Classification of Secondary School Courses (CSSC) course taxonomy that the National Center for Education Statistics uses to categorize all courses in their transcript studies program.[1]

While existing taxonomies can be used as valuable tools in the development of an operational definition of a concept, they are not a panacea. It is important to be selective and judicious when selecting or creating the categories of a taxonomy that will comprise the operational definition. Drawing on an existing taxonomy without critically examining its construction could result in the development of an operational definition that is not representative of the concept that the indicator is designed to measure. For example, suppose that an indicator is being developed to measure the amount of crime and disorder in schools. Further suppose that the operational definition draws upon a taxonomy that is composed of seven categories of crime and lawbreaking, and that two of these categories are moving violations and parking tickets. Including these categories in the operational definition of school crime will result in an inflated estimate of the true amount of school crime; most people would not consider the accrual of speeding tickets or parking violations to be instances of "school crime." Additionally, taxonomies can change. For example, student course taking will change as new courses are required or developed. Clearly, then, taxonomies are useful tools in the development of operational definitions, but their construction and composition need to be carefully analyzed when being used for such a purpose.

While the use of existing taxonomies represents one method of developing an operational definition, they are certainly not the sole scheme for accomplishing this task. The development of an operational definition can be informed by many other factors. For example, previous work that has established accepted definitions and practices often plays an influential role in developing an operational definition. Relying on established operational definitions with which people are already familiar lends an air of quality to the indicator. It also eliminates the need to demonstrate that the operational definition validly represents the concept that the indicator is designed to measure.

The goals of the organization developing the indicator are also likely to factor into the process of developing an operational definition. As we will demonstrate in a later chapter, operationally defining a concept in different manners can lead to different results and substantive conclusions, a fact that policy organizations and government agencies know well and certainly consider when developing an operational definition for an indicator. As an example, suppose that a teachers' union and a market-oriented education reform organization were each developing an indicator to measure the same concept, such as teacher quality. It is very likely that the two organizations would operationalize the concept of teacher quality in quite different manners.

Regardless of the factors that influence the development of an operational definition, this task is clearly one of the most difficult, yet important, stages in the indicator creation process. It sets the tone for the rest of the process and plays a large role in determining the substantive conclusions that will be taken away from the indicator by policy makers and analysts. This section has described many of the practical aspects involved in developing an operational definition, but there are many technical matters that must be considered as well. We discuss these issues extensively in a later section of this chapter.

Concrete Measurement

Once an operational definition has been established, the next task involves deciding how the operational concept should be measured. That is, how exactly are you going to ask the question on a survey or define an item on an administrative form? This is where the concept becomes a reality. It is the process where one collects an observation that relates to the concept at hand. It is from this observation that we produce indicator values. While we present the development of an operational definition and decisions of measurement as separate stages of the indicator creation process, these stages often take place simultaneously in practice. It would be useless to employ an operational definition that is very difficult or impossible to measure. Decisions of measurement must be made under a variety of considerations, both practical and technical. We begin by describing the practical factors that enter into measurement decisions; we cover the more technical considerations of both operationalization and measurement in a later section of this chapter.

There are two practical issues to consider when making decisions about measuring an operational definition. The close relationship between the development of an operational definition and issues of measurement will be apparent in the discussion of these practical considerations. First, it is necessary to determine where the information and data required to measure the concept will come from—Who will you ask? Second, it is vital to determine the precise information or data that will be obtained, as well as the precise wording of the data or information request and the method of administering that request—What will you ask? How will you ask it? Each of these issues is very important when determining how to measure an operational definition, and the following two sections address them in a comprehensive manner.

Who will you ask?

Determining the source of the information is the first practical issue to address. For every operational definition, there are always multiple ways to obtain the data and information necessary to measure the concept. Two of the most common sources of data are administrative records and self-reports.

Administrative records. Generally, administrative records are kept by institutions or government entities as a product of an administrative activity or for the purpose of complying with some sort of data reporting requirements. For example, schools maintain teacher and staff payroll information and student coursework and grades. Similarly, schools are required to track student attendance for purposes of school funding; as a result, schools keep a close record of attendance. In another example, school districts are mandated by law to report the proportion of teachers who are "highly qualified," as defined by the No Child Left Behind Act of 2001. Accordingly, districts maintain detailed information on teachers' credentials, including their academic degrees, their college majors, their state certifications, and other characteristics.

The main benefits of administrative records are threefold: Records are readily available, they are comprehensive, and they have standardized data elements. First, administrative records are usually available and simply need to be accessed. Student transcripts, for example, are a running collection of student coursework, grades, and credits earned. These records are the cornerstone to all school record systems and are maintained regularly since they serve both internal and external functions. Internally, transcripts are used to determine student transition to higher grades, course schedules based on past performance, and when students satisfy graduation requirements. Externally, transcripts serve as evidence for postsecondary admissions and labor market employment requirements. Given the value of this documentation, schools devote a lot of effort to keeping them up-to-date and accurate.

Second, records are comprehensive, and generally contain information for every individual in a given population. Returning to our example, student transcripts contain information for every student in a district, not just for a selected sample of students. In more technical terms, this is referred to as having universe data or a census.

Third, administrative data are arguably less susceptible to erroneous measurements given the standardized reporting practice. Administrative records are often verified by third parties or rely on other pieces of information to ensure accuracy. So, for example, school attendance records are not collected by asking students whether they attend class or not. Rather, teachers observe and make note of which students are in class and which are not. While teachers certainly make some errors when taking attendance, this process likely returns more accurate results than asking students about their attendance records.

The main drawback to administrative data is the fact that it is often limited in scope, which can significantly constrain the number of topics for which it can be used. Administrative records are generally maintained to meet specific reporting requirements, and educational institutions rarely collect and maintain information that extends beyond meeting the minimum requirements. Such limited data collection practices are completely understandable. Educators and administrators are often overburdened, with free time, resources, and support staff coming at a premium. Collecting data to meet reporting requirements represents one more task that they have to fit into their already hectic schedules. As a result, they collect the minimum amount of information and data that will result in compliance with the reporting requirements. That being said, the limit of scope for administrative records collection can vary across schools. For example, some schools have very detailed transcripts that include student coursework, grades, grade point averages (GPAs), class rank, health records, disciplinary actions, and college admission tests. Others may simply have course titles and grades. Most do not have measures of a student's poverty status or other parental information. Similarly, the recording of course grades may vary across schools. For example, it is not uncommon for some schools to modify a student's transcript if they retake a course. If a student fails a course and retakes it the following semester, some schools remove the failing course and only report the passing grade, other include both courses, and still others will include both courses but only count the retaken course toward the GPA.

The practical consequence of the limited scope of administrative data is that it may not be perfectly aligned with the operational definition that has been developed. As an example, researchers and policy makers are often interested in the amount of time students spend volunteering and the type of volunteering they perform (Hart, Donnelly, Youniss, & Atkins, 2007). Quite often schools require students to perform service learning or community service to graduate. It is likely that many schools will have some documentation that the service hours were fulfilled, but the ability to use that measure as the basis for an indicator that purports to describe the quantity and quality of student volunteering experiences will be limited. Even if the student's record has additional information about the number of total hours volunteered, detailed information about the quality of the experiences will be lacking. While this scenario is hypothetical, it is illustrative of many real scenarios where administrative data do not perfectly align with the operational definition of an indicator's objective.

Another concern with administrative records is the lack of standardized data elements across units. That is, even if a concept is measured on the same scale, inherent differences in how it is reported can result in issues of comparability. Returning to transcripts, the grade point average is a typical measure produced by schools based on student performance. However, the standards used to assign grades and construct grade point averages vary across schools. These disparities have students and parents in some schools concerned about fairness (Mathews, 2007). For example, a student scoring 90 or better on a 100-point scale receives an A in Montgomery County, Maryland, and the District of Columbia, but just a few miles away in Fairfax County, Virginia, the same student would need a 94 or better to receive an A. Further, as is often the case, students who take Advanced Placement (AP), International Baccalaureate, or other college-level courses receive bonus points for tackling more difficult work. However, in one district students are awarded 1 point and in others only a half point is awarded, introducing another distortion. A final concern is that even with an adoption of similar grading systems, some students may encounter more difficult teachers who are harder graders or courses with the same titles that cover very different content. So a student taking Algebra 1 in one school district may cover more difficult and advanced concepts and have a teacher who is a very hard grader, awarding only a few As. In another school, students in Algebra 1 may be exposed to only basic concepts, with most students awarded As and Bs. Such content and standards disparities are very hard to detect in administrative records.

Self-reports. The second common source of information used to construct indicator measures is self-reported data. Perhaps not surprisingly, the strengths of measures derived from self-reports tend to correspond to the weaknesses of measures obtained from administrative data. Specifically, the strongest aspect of the self-reported approach is the potential to elicit data that are strongly aligned with the operational definition of an indicator. The primary disadvantages of self-report are rooted in the respondent's ability to recall information and bias. Depending on whom you ask and when, you can get very different responses. Respondents may have a difficult time recalling events or precise details. Other respondents may provide inaccurate information from selective memories or willfully provide wrong answers.

To illustrate the impressive ability of self-reports to align measures with an operational definition, consider an indicator on high school guidance counseling published in NCES's *Condition of Education* (Wirt et al., 2004). A quick read reveals that the conceptual definition of this indicator involved describing high school guidance staff and the goals of guidance programs (conceptual definition). The concept of describing the high school guidance staff was operationalized as the number of students per guidance counselor, while the concept of describing the goals of guidance programs was operationalized by four goals: helping students plan and prepare for their work roles after high school, helping students with personal growth and development, helping students plan and prepare for postsecondary schooling, and helping students with their academic achievement in high school (operational definition). NCES decided to measure these operational concepts with items that were asked of the lead guidance counselor at a nationally representative sample of schools. The decision to measure the goals of guidance programs using self-reports allowed the creators of the indicator to develop items that were closely aligned with the operational definition, a task that would be very difficult to accomplish if administrative data were used in the development of the indicator.

While self-reports can provide valuable information, they are not flawless. Reports of specific events can vary dramatically depending upon the source of the self-report. For example, in a recent survey, parents, students, and staff showed significant disagreement on measures of safety and climate

Table 2.1. Percentage of students, parents, and staff who agreed with school safety and climate question, by school level: 2009

Elementary Schools	Student	Parent	Staff
Feel safe at school/safe place.	90	95	97
In this school, students teasing other students is a problem.	69	19	39
In this school, students bullying other students is a problem.	61	20	30
In this school, drug use is a problem.	31	4	3
In this school, alcohol use is a problem.	31	4	3

High Schools	Student	Parent	Staff
Feel safe at school/safe place.	78	86	90
In this school, students teasing other students is a problem.	55	15	44
In this school, students bullying other students is a problem.	47	25	38
In this school, drug use is a problem.	56	34	54
In this school, alcohol use is a problem.	50	34	51

Source. Data taken from Montgomery County Public Schools (MCPS). (2009). Student and parent 2008-09 survey of school environment. Rockville, MD: Author. Retrieved March 9, 2010, from http://sharedaccountability.mcpsprimetime.org/SurveyResults/

within their schools (Montgomery County, 2009). For example, 4% of elementary school parents and 3% of staff agreed with the statement that drug use was a problem in the school compared to 31% of the students (see Table 2.1). When we look at high schools, staff and students are more congruent with 54% of staff and 56% of students reporting drug use as a schoolwide problem, but parents were lower at 34%. For bullying, only 20% of elementary school parents felt that this was a problem in school compared to 30% of staff and 61% of elementary students. While it certainly may be useful to highlight the perceived differences between these sources, the general principle for survey research is that, for a variety of reasons, perceptions and experiences will vary by source. Care must be taken when choosing the most appropriate respondent, with the study's purpose, objectives, and costs dictating the most appropriate source for information. In addition, it is generally felt that the source most closely related to the event or item at hand is likely to provide better-quality responses.

A number of studies have examined the accuracy of student self-reports of performance indicators such as grade point averages, test scores, and coursework (see Kuncel, Crede, & Thomas, 2005, for a nice review of the literature). Many studies must rely on student self-reports versus official transcripts or records because administrative sources of data are unavailable or costly to collect and process. In general, students tend to overreport their performance, but these errors tend to be modest. However, research has found significant upward bias for low-performing students. The self-reports of high-performing students are quite similar to school-reported performance. For college students, self-reported GPAs were generally more reliable compared to the self-reported high school GPAs of students. This may be simply due to the selection of higher-performing students in college. Beyond performance level, there are very few other student characteristics related to reporting errors. While our understanding of the errors associated with surveys and self-reports is rather long and detailed, little systematic data are available about the limitations or error structure related to administrative records, especially in education.[2]

Of course, comparing student self-reports to official administrative records as the "correct" value assumes a high level of accuracy in these records. However, as we described earlier, administrative records are prone to multiple sources of error, including recording errors, variability across reporting units, missing data, data entry delays and mistakes, and processing errors (Iezzoni, 1997). In addition, depending on the measure, administrative data are prone to manipulation.[3] Roy and Mishel (2008) examine the reliability of school enrollment data and demonstrate inconsistencies, unexplained volatility, and other data problems. This is not surprising, as there are very few, if any, auditing systems in place to identify reporting errors as information is passed from the schools to districts to state education agencies and finally to the federal government collection systems. In any case, the use of administrative records proves to have as many challenges in terms of reliability and validity as self-reported sources of information, but the types and magnitude of errors may differ.

In the field of education, most indicators could be constructed using information from any of a variety of sources. For example, let's take school crime. There are multiple sources of information about the level and type of crime in schools. One can gather information from principals or student records, from teachers, or from the students themselves. You might even consider asking the local police about the number of criminal events on campus. The choice is critical in this case since there are good reasons why each will, and should, provide a different estimate. Each source has a number of social filters related to the reporting of any criminal event (Skogan, 1974, 1984). Beginning at the time of the event, a number of factors must align to have the event recorded as an official statistic. Generally, the victim or bystander must recognize that a criminal act has occurred and then make the decision to call the police or other official. In schools, this other official may be a teacher, principal, or guidance counselor. These officials may then choose to call the police or handle the matter through a different means. For many serious crimes school officials must contact authorities, but for many other acts they have a great deal of discretion. Once the police are involved, officers will gather information and decide on whether there is evidence that a crime did occur and then classify the type of crime. Often students or the general public are not intimately familiar with the law and may confuse crime types,[4] or police may only find evidence for a certain type of crime when the victim claims otherwise. Depending on the nature of each of these reporting stages, one would get very different counts and perspectives on crime in school. Principals and police officers may only come across the most serious events that get reported up the line. Lesser events like fighting, drug-use, or bullying may only reach the students, bystanders, or teachers. More serious crimes like homicide are most likely perceived by all, but these are rare events and in most schools nonexistent. On the flip side, principals will be more likely to know about the details of every crime that was reported to school officials, whereas students will generally know what happens to them or in their immediate social network. Some crimes such as sexual assault, drug use, and theft are not as visible to the public and often reported through private lines of communication.

This example illustrates that the source of the self-report has the potential to have a significant effect on the substantive conclusions that may be drawn from an indicator. In sum, there are a variety of issues that must be confronted and questions that must be answered when deciding whether to use data collected from administrative records or self-reports as the basis for an indicator. Both sources have a unique set of benefits and drawbacks, and the ultimate decision to go with one over the other should be made after carefully considering the appropriateness of each potential source for the situation at hand. If it is important for a measure to be closely aligned with the operational definition and it would be desirable to collect additional information of interest, then self-reported data from sample surveys may be preferable. On the flip side, if it is important to have a very accurate measure of the concept, then administrative records may be the best source of data.

Other concerns about data quality relate to the use of information from administrative or official records versus self-reports. Should we be comfortable using student self-reports of their grades, coursework, or other performance indicators, or are administrative records a better source? Similar issues arise with respect to asking teachers about salaries or credentials. Decisions need to be made regarding whether we should rely on their reports, or whether it would be better to go to administrative records for this type of information. The resolution to this decision depends on the context. It is obviously more expensive to get both sources of information, so when a choice needs to be made, most often we go with self-reports. The reason is that administrative records are limited in their scope, and when we rely on administrative records alone, we lose out on important analytical variables or characteristics that are not captured in these records. For example, we might have very good records on teacher salaries when we access the district payrolls. However, this high quality comes at a cost, since we have little to no information about other sources of teacher income earned from outside activities. Knowing something about other sources of income, total household income, and the number of people living in the household may be crucial for the purposes of an indicator.

What will you ask and how will you ask it?

After settling on the source for information, attention turns to developing the instruments and mode of data collection that will be used to elicit the information of interest. This is the process of implementing the operational definition and generating observations and data. In the case of administrative records, this issue is largely a settled matter. The instruments, items, and formats used to collect administrative data cannot be altered to fit the specific purposes of an indicator that is being developed. The researcher is restricted to the available information. When administrative data have been selected as the mode of data collection, there is an element of "What you see is what you get" with respect to the information that is available for inclusion in the indicator.

What will you ask? There is much more flexibility in what can be asked when a researcher elects to use self-reports through surveys as the mode of data collection. In these cases the individual or organization constructing the indicator has a large amount of discretion over the content of the survey and the design of the survey instrument. For example, the developers could decide whether to measure the operational definition with a single item or multiple items. Similarly, development of a survey instrument allows designers to develop an operational definition with several dimensions that can all be directly measured using items on the survey instrument.

Let's take an example of school engagement. This concept has become a centerpiece for research dealing with academic achievement and dropping out of high school. Students who are not engaged in school activities are more likely to either do poorly in school or leave altogether. But just what exactly is school engagement? A simple answer could be how involved a student is in his or her school. This could be measured by simply asking, How many days has the student missed school? Presumably, students who are actively engaged in school will have good attendance records. This is a mea-

sure that surely most schools keep in administrative records. But most researchers would recognize several limitations with such an indicator. In their
review of the research literature, Fredricks, Blumenfeld, and Paris (2004)
identify three types of school engagement: behavioral, emotional, and cognitive. Behavioral includes positive conduct (absence of disciplinary problems), normative behaviors (follow rules), contributing to class discussion,
and involvement in extracurricular activities. Emotional school engagement
relates to classroom interest, feelings of belonging, attitudes toward school-
work, and boredom, among others. Cognitive engagement focuses on the
student's academic environment, problem solving, and investment in learning. Within the three types of school engagement—behavioral, emotional,
and cognitive—each separate component can be observed in ways that are
unlikely to be gleaned from an administrative record. Instead, researchers
would be better off developing a survey that contained items inquiring about
each aspect of school engagement and relying on self-reports to generate an
indicator on the topic.

In general, it is preferable to have multiple measures of an operational
definition. This is especially true in the case of complex indicators—those
that combine multiple topics into a single indicator—such as school climate
or college readiness. To illustrate the benefits of multiple measures, consider
an indicator that measures school climate. One option for measuring the
operational definition of school climate would be to simply ask respondents
to rate the climate of their school on a scale that ranges from 1 to 5. While
this approach possesses the virtue of simplicity, it also has a number of potential drawbacks. For example, different respondents may consider entirely
different factors when answering the item. Some respondents may base their
evaluation of the school climate on issues like the number of fights and
violence at school. Others may consider class disruptions. Clearly, asking
respondents simply to rate the school climate may return evaluations that
are not based on a common factor. As a result, it would be preferable to
ask respondents concrete questions about specific factors that comprise the
climate of a school, such as disciplinary policies, student behavior, drug or
alcohol use, graffiti, and any other factors included in the operational definition of the indicator. Then the responses to these concrete questions could
be compiled to construct an index of school climate.

This example also illustrates another important point, namely, when determining what to ask, it is generally preferable to develop items that are
concrete, rather than abstract, in nature. For example, for a question inquiring about student disruptions, it would be preferable to ask respondents to
estimate the number of class disruptions in a given period of time, rather
than to rate how large of a problem class disruptions are on a scale from 1

to 5. Asking respondents to answer a concrete question with a specific point of reference generally returns more accurate and reliable responses.

Administrative records and self-reports are just two sources of information. Other sources include direct observation by interviewers and third-party accounts of student behavior (such as from parents and teachers). For instance, the state of school facilities can be assessed by third-party observers during visitations (Planty & DeVoe, 2005), and teachers are often seen as an objective source for student behavior (Dee, 2005; Ehrenberg, Goldhaber, & Brewer, 1995). The advantages and disadvantages of third-party reports are similar to self-report surveys.

How will you ask it? A critical component of asking questions involves determining the precise wording of the data or information request and the method of administering that request. Put another way: How will you ask it? This is an additional source of complexity that indicator developers must confront when attempting to measure an operational definition. To begin with, developers of an indicator must consider issues of item composition and survey instrument development. It has been repeatedly demonstrated that the specific wording of a question and the ordering of items on a survey instrument can have a substantial effect on the answers given by survey respondents (Groves et al., 2009; Sudman & Bradburn, 1974; Sudman, Bradburn, & Schwarz, 1996). Items must be developed and worded in a manner that accurately measures the operational definition of an indicator. Successfully completing this task requires a good deal of skill and thought. Similarly, the ordering of questions on survey instruments can also influence respondents, so survey developers need to be careful to construct the survey in a manner that does not systematically influence the answers of respondents. In short, items should be worded, and survey instruments should be developed, in a manner that produces valid and reliable answers from survey respondents, issues that will be discussed later in this chapter.

In addition to being cognizant of issues associated with item wording and survey instrument development, indicator developers must consider the method with which the data collection instruments will be administered. There are a wide variety of manners in which a survey instrument can be administered. Some of the most common methods include mail surveys, telephone interviews, in-person interviews, and, more frequently in recent years, online surveys. Each of these modes of administration has a unique composition of characteristics that make them more amenable to some purposes than others.

Mail surveys are popular for many institutions and organizations because of the relatively low costs associated with their administration. Generally, the main costs associated with this form of administration are printing and postage. The downsides associated with mail surveys are that they often have quite low response rates and it is not always clear as to who actually responds. Often, potential respondents receive the survey in the mail and set it aside, intending to fill it out later, but end up failing to return it. The low response rates associated with mail surveys can cause biased results because the respondents who returned the survey are unlikely to be representative of all the potential respondents to whom the survey was mailed. This method of administration is not uncommon in nonprofit organizations. For example, the Center for Education Reform administers their Annual Survey of America's Charter Schools through the mail. Mail surveys can also be found in the repertoire of government agencies; for example, the School Survey on Crime and Safety is administered as a mail survey with a telephone follow-up.

Telephone interviews have long been a common method of data collection, especially in the realm of government surveys. Data for several large, nationally representative surveys—most notably the National Household Education Survey—that serve as the basis of education indicators developed by the federal government are collected via telephone interviewing. Telephone interviews are generally more expensive to conduct than mail surveys because individuals must be paid to make the calls. A second potential drawback to this method of administration is the fact that individuals without phones are not sampled. This problem has become more complex in recent years with the explosive growth in cell phone usage, where numbers are not listed, do not match local area codes, or are otherwise inaccessible (Blumberg & Luke, 2009). On the other hand, surveys administered via telephone are often able to obtain higher response rates than mail surveys, although response rates for telephone surveys have been declining in recent years.

In-person interviews are undoubtedly the most expensive method of survey administration because interviewers have to travel to respondents' residences to administer the survey. However, this form of survey administration usually generates the highest response rates and responses with the highest degrees of reliability and validity. Trained interviewers are able to standardize the data collection process by closely following design protocol to eliminate error. Standardization is especially important when administering timed assessments. For these reasons, many large-scale surveys related to education that are conducted by the government are administered using in-person interviews. For example, the Current Population Survey, the Early Childhood Longitudinal Survey, the High School Longitudinal Survey of 2009, and a number of other data collection efforts are conducted—in whole or in part—using in-person interviews.

Online surveys—collecting data through the Internet—are undoubtedly the least expensive of the four major options discussed here, but due to their relative youth there is substantial uncertainty associated with several aspects of this data collection regime. Most notably, it is unclear how well samples obtained from online surveys represent the larger population. For this and other reasons, the use of online surveys to collect data used for indicator creation is relatively rare.

However, the Internet has been an incredibly useful tool for the purposes of centralizing administrative data. Today, local jurisdictions such as school districts and states can submit required data and information to the U.S. Department of Education using the Internet. Indeed, much of the information available through the Common Core of Data, a massive database maintained by the National Center for Education Statistics, is collected in this manner. Similarly, school districts can often submit required information to their state departments of education using Internet forms. The Internet has undeniably increased the speed and efficiency with which administrative data can be centralized and subsequently be made available to researchers and the general public.

The essential goal in the development of any indicator is to create the highest-quality product in a given time frame within a set budget. It is often the case that an indicator could be improved with a bigger budget or more time. For example, with a bigger budget, the data used to construct the indicator could involve very detailed questionnaires. Similarly, with more time, different question wordings and survey instrument designs could be pilot-tested multiple times to determine the optimal question wording and instrument design. In reality, however, time and money are limited resources, and all decisions relevant to the construction of an indicator must be made within these constraints.

CONSIDERATIONS OF RELIABILITY AND VALIDITY

To this point, we have demonstrated that the construction of an indicator is a multistep process that requires making a series of substantive decisions with respect to definition—both conceptual and operational—and measurement. Some of these decisions are constrained by factors such as time, money, data, and available resources; but other decisions, such as the choice of an operational definition or the development of measurement instruments, often require judgment calls that are based on a reasoned assessment by the creator of an indicator. Confronting such difficult and important decisions raises a couple of questions: Upon what considerations should these judgments about definition and measurement be based? Is there an accepted framework that can guide the development of a strategy for defining and measuring the concept underlying an indicator?

Fortunately, there are a number of accepted criteria that can, and should, inform decisions related to definition and measurement. Specifically, definitional and measurement decisions should be based on the twin considerations of reliability and validity. Basing decisions about definition and measurement on these criteria will likely enhance the quality of the resulting indicator, which will permit it to be more readily accepted as providing an accurate depiction of the status of the topic it purports to describe. As a result, an indicator based on these criteria is likely to have a larger impact in the policy arena than an indicator that only considers issues of reliability and validity in a haphazard manner. This section of the chapter explores the criteria of reliability and validity in greater detail.

Validity

Every indicator should strive to provide valid operational definitions and measures of the concept it purports to describe. In very general terms, *validity* is the extent to which the operational definition and measurement strategy employed in an indicator captures what it is trying to capture (Asher, 2001; King, Keohane, & Verba, 1994). Because the concept of validity is so broad, scholars have developed a number of distinct dimensions, or aspects, of validity. We discuss six of them—face validity, content validity, criterion validity, construct validity, external validity, and statistical validity—in the paragraphs that follow, and provide contextual examples for each dimension of validity that we address. While each of these dimensions of validity is conceptually distinct in nature, taken together they comprise the broader notion of validity.

The first test of validity that every operational definition and measurement strategy must pass is face validity. *Face validity* refers to whether, at first glance, the operational definition and measurement strategy used in the indicator make sense. That is, does it seem plausible that they could result in an indicator that accurately describes the concept it purports to describe? Most of the time, published indicators have, at the very minimum, reasonable levels of face validity. As a result, published examples of indicators with low face validity are rare. However, less extreme examples of indicators with questionable face validity can be found: for example the debate over high school graduation rates. Larry Mishel, a labor economist, became very skeptical of recent claims that high schools graduate only two-thirds of all students and only about half of minority students, and that graduation rates have been declining in recent times (Mishel, 2006). Such claims were inconsistent with Mishel's economic data, which actually indicated that the proportion of individuals in the labor market who had a high school degree has been increasing. Such a finding would imply that dropout rates have been declining, not rising, over time. After investigating the education estimates, Mishel demonstrated that the potential source of difference was primarily a problem with the quality of data used to generate the high school graduation rates. The graduation rate debate continues, but the point is that diverging trends may suggest more subtle concerns over face validity. Likewise, researchers often compare previous-year estimates to current-year estimates as a form of face validity. Using the assumption that indicators tend not to have wild year-to-year fluctuations, large annual swings in an estimate are more suggestive of a problem with the data collection process rather than a reflection of reality. Consider the school crime and safety indicator example we employed earlier.[5] In this indicator, school crime is operationally defined as the number of violent incidents, theft/larceny incidents, and other incidents, which include possession of a weapon, illegal drug or alcohol use, and vandalism. This operational definition is measured through a survey administered to school principals. Taken together, we would rate this indicator as having high face validity; the combination of the operational definition and measurement strategy could produce an accurate portrayal of school crime and safety.

So what would an indicator with low face validity look like? Suppose that the indicator of school crime and safety operationally defined the concept as the level of truancy within a school. Further suppose that the indicator measured the operational definition by sending a survey to a sample of parents within each school in the sample of schools that inquired about the truancy habits of their child. Such an operational definition and measurement strategy would hopefully never be employed in a published indicator, but it provides an illustration of an indicator with low face validity. A quick glance at the operational definition reveals that it is unlikely to provide an accurate portrayal of the true level of crime and safety within schools. Similarly, the hypothetical measurement strategy of asking parents also seems problematic; children are unlikely to fully inform their parents about their truancy habits. It is important to remember that an indicator does not either have low face validity or high face validity, but operates along a continuum that ranges from low to high. We chose examples at the extremities of this continuum for the purposes of illustrating the concept of face validity.

Related to, but distinct from, face validity is content validity. *Content validity* refers to the extent to which the operational definition and measurement strategy employed in an indicator reflect all aspects of the concept it purports to describe (Carmines & Zeller, 1991). Although this dimension of validity is applicable to a broad range of topics, it most commonly arises with respect to standardized testing. Suppose an indicator was being developed that is operationally defined as measuring the mathematics achievement of sixth graders. But suppose further that the test used to measure mathematics achievement only contained items that required the students to solve multiplication and addition problems; there were no items that tapped students' knowledge of fractions, decimals, or any other mathematical concept besides multiplication and addition. Because the standardized test used to measure mathematics achievement only measured two aspects of mathematics knowledge, it would not have high content validity.

While content validity is most commonly considered to be a measure of how well the composition of a standardized test covers the content area it is designed to assess, the concept of content validity can also be applied more generally. For example, consider the school crime and safety example we have discussed above. As described earlier, this indicator measured school crime and safety by assessing the number of violent incidents, theft/larceny incidents, and other incidents, which include possession of a weapon, illegal drug or alcohol use, and vandalism. Because the indicator measures most, and possibly all, of the aspects of school crime and safety that might be considered consequential, it would likely be judged as having high content validity. Consider, however, a hypothetical scenario where the indicator measured only one or two aspects of school crime and safety, such as illegal drug and alcohol use, and completely ignored other relevant domains. If the indicator were constructed in this manner, it would not have a high level of content validity.

These examples make clear that face validity and content validity are distinct, but clearly related, concepts. An indicator that does not have high content validity is also likely to lack high face validity. However, the two dimensions of validity are not identical; an indicator might have a relatively higher level of face validity than content validity, or vice versa. There are no formal measures to estimate the precise levels of concept and face validity; rather, these are based on subjective evaluations.

The third dimension of validity we will explore is criterion or criterion-related validity. *Criterion validity* is mainly applicable to newly developed operational definitions and measurement strategies. Criterion validity is comparative in nature and involves demonstrating that one operational definition and measurement strategy—usually a newly developed one—performs similarly to another operational definition and measurement strategy that has been proven to provide a valid portrayal of the concept addressed in the indicator. As a hypothetical example, consider the indicator described above that was being developed to measure the mathematics achievement of sixth graders. The vast majority of indicators that purport to measure achievement do so through the administration of a standardized test, a measurement strategy that is generally regarded as a valid one. Suppose, however, that the administration and analysis of a standardized test was unworkable for this indicator because the requisite fiscal resources were not available. As a result, the developers of the indicator have decided to use student grades in their sixth-grade math class as the measure of mathematics achievement because it is easily available from transcripts and inexpensive to obtain. Criterion validity would involve demonstrating that an indicator that uses student grades as a measure of mathematics achievement produces conclusions that are substantively similar to the conclusions that would be produced by an indicator that measures achievement using a standardized test.

Practically, issues of criterion validity only need to be considered when a new or untraditional operational definition or measurement strategy is being used to describe a concept. If the consumer of an indicator confronts a situation where a fairly common concept is being operationally defined and measured in an uncommon or untraditional manner, it is advisable to look for evidence that the new definition and measure has been demonstrated to perform similarly to more traditional definitions and measures. That is, it is advisable to look for evidence that it has criterion validity.

The fourth dimension of validity that we describe here is construct validity. When people refer to "validity" in a general sense, they are usually referring to construct validity. In its essence, *construct validity* refers to the extent to which the operational definition and measurement strategy align with the conceptual definition. Simply put, does the indicator measure what it is trying to measure? As an example of the concept of construct validity, consider our running example of the indicator that describes the status of school crime and safety. As noted earlier, this indicator measures school crime and safety as the number of violent incidents, theft/larceny incidents, and other incidents, which include possession of a weapon, illegal drug or alcohol use, and vandalism. Most people would agree that this operational definition and measurement strategy will result in an accurate portrayal of the concept of school crime and safety. Consider, however, the hypothetical scenario, also presented above, where school crime and safety is operationally defined and measured as the number of incidents of illegal alcohol and drug use within the school. While drug and alcohol use certainly represents an aspect of school crime and safety, most people likely believe that such a measure does not provide a high-quality representation of the concept of school crime and safety. As a result, such an indicator would have low levels of construct validity.

As a second hypothetical example, consider an indicator that is designed to measure computer use in the classroom. Ideally, the indicator would rely on a survey of teachers that asked how often they used the computers in their classroom. However, budgetary constraints prevent the developers of the indicator from designing and administering such a survey, and they instead rely on administrative data that contain information on the number of computers in each classroom. As a result, computer use in the classroom is operationally defined and measured as the number of computers in the classroom. While the number of computers in a classroom is useful information, it is not likely that this operational definition and measurement strategy provides an accurate portrayal of the concept of computer use in the classroom, which results in a low level of construct validity.

Because construct validity is perhaps the most general dimension of validity, it should not come as a surprise that it is possesses some connections to the other dimensions of validity. Specifically, an indicator with low levels of content validity will have low levels of construct validity; if an operational definition measures only a portion of the concept being described (content validity), then it is unlikely to provide a high-quality representation of the concept (construct validity). Similarly, an indicator with low construct validity will also likely possess low face validity. If an operational definition and measurement strategy do not result in an accurate portrayal of the concept being described, the indicator is unlikely to pass the smell test.

The fifth dimension of validity that should be considered when assessing an indicator is external validity. *External validity* is the extent to which the estimates in an indicator are representative of the actual status of the topic in a broader, defined population. External validity can be affected by several factors, but perhaps the most influential determinant of external validity is the alignment between the composition of the sample from which the estimate presented in the indicator is constructed and the population that the estimate is supposed to represent. Put simply, external validity is determined by how well the information used to create the indicator represents the broader population. The following two examples illustrate a hypothetical indicator with low and high levels of external validity, respectively.

First, consider the example of the indicator designed to measure the mathematics achievement of sixth graders. Suppose that the indicator is designed to describe the mathematics achievement of all sixth graders within a given state. However, the designers of the indicator estimated sixth-grade mathematics achievement using an exam that was only administered to sixth graders in four wealthy, suburban schools. The results from this assessment administration were then used as the estimate of statewide mathematics achievement. An indicator constructed in this manner would have low external validity; it is unlikely that the results of a mathematics assessment administered to students in wealthy, suburban schools do a good job of representing the level of mathematics achievement for all students within a state.

Alternatively, again consider an indicator designed to measure the statewide mathematics achievement of sixth graders. This time, however, the developers of the indicator administer the assessment to a different sample. Specifically, they compile a list of all schools in the state and then randomly choose a sampling of schools from the list and administer the assessment in those schools. The results of the assessment administered to this sample of schools are then used as the estimate of statewide sixth-grade mathematics achievement. An indicator based on this measurement scheme will have a high level of external validity; by choosing a random selection of schools the assessment is likely to be administered to a sample of students that is broadly representative of the statewide student population.

It is important to note that simply distributing a survey or assessment to a representative sample of the target population does not guarantee high levels of external validity. Even if a survey or assessment is distributed to a sample that represents the population, it could be the case that not everyone will complete the survey or assessment. If the people who complete the survey or assessment are somehow unlike the people who do not complete the survey—perhaps they are more motivated—then that represents a threat to external validity. In sum, the main consideration in external validity involves assessing the extent to which the sample from which an indicator is constructed represents the population that the indicator hopes to describe.

The last dimension of validity that we discuss here is statistical validity. *Statistical validity* refers to whether the estimates presented in an indicator were produced using the most appropriate statistical procedure. As we briefly noted in Chapter 1 and will describe in greater detail in a later chapter, indicators can often employ a variety of different statistics to produce the final estimate. For example, consider our hypothetical indicator that describes average statewide mathematics achievement of sixth graders. The developers of the indicator could use any of several accepted and well-known measures of central tendency to measure average mathematics achievement. Specifically, they could choose between the mean, median, and modal scores on the assessment to represent average achievement. In this case, measuring average achievement with either the mean or median score would have high statistical validity; these statistics are generally well-accepted methods of representing average test score achievement. Using the modal score would have less statistical validity. Using the modal value is rarely an appropriate representation of central tendency. Overall, the best way to assess the statistical validity of an indicator is to look at other indicators that purport to describe the same or similar topics, and identify the statistic used to produce the estimate. If both indicators use the same statistic, you can generally be confident in the statistical validity of the indicator.

In this section we have identified and described six dimensions of validity that should be considered throughout the indicator creation process. While each of these dimensions of validity is conceptually distinct, they are undoubtedly related in practice. An indicator that performs poorly on one dimension of validity is also likely to perform poorly on one or more other measures. Conceptually, the *overall validity* of an indicator can be thought of as the sum of the performance of the indicator on each of these six dimensions. Unfortunately, there is no clear and simple method for assessing the performance of an indicator on each dimension of validity discussed earlier; assessments of an indicator's validity are certainly subjective in nature, but such evaluations can be based on well-accepted and standard criteria. The previous paragraphs provide guidance, and a number of examples, that can aid in such assessments, but in the end it is the responsibility of the consumer to reach a well-reasoned, educated judgment about the overall validity of an indicator.

Reliability

The previous section makes it clear that definitional and measurement decisions need to be based on considerations of validity, but validity is certainly not the only factor that needs to be considered. The concept of reliability is also an important determinant of the quality of an indicator and needs to be considered when deciding how to operationally define and measure a concept. At the most basic level, *reliability* is the extent to which a given operational definition and measurement strategy yields consistent estimates of the concept it is designed to measure when it is administered multiple times. Put very simply, reliability refers to the consistency of a measure.

To illustrate the concept of reliability, consider the case of the high school guidance counseling indicator that we discussed earlier. To reach their estimates of the goals of high school guidance counseling departments across the country, the developers of the indicator administered a questionnaire to a nationally representative sample of guidance counselors. The questionnaire contained a number of items that inquired about the goals that the guidance counseling offices emphasized. To have a high degree of reliability, the questionnaire would need to elicit the same, or similar, responses if individuals filled it out multiple times under similar conditions. Put in context, the questionnaire should result in guidance counselors describing their goals in a similar, and ideally identical, manner if they were administered the questionnaire multiple times.

This example demonstrates one main type of reliability that we discuss in this chapter: test-retest reliability. *Test-retest reliability* refers to the degree of stability in the estimates of a concept resulting from administration of a data collection instrument—whether it is a standardized test or a survey questionnaire—if it is administered to the same individual at different points in time. Test-retest reliability is very important for indicators that attempt to describe student achievement, a concept that is often measured using standardized tests. For a standardized test to provide a high-quality estimate of student achievement, it is vital that the assessment provide a consistently accurate measure of students' ability, such as mathematics ability. Because a student's true mathematics ability likely does not change much over a short period of time, students should obtain similar scores on the assessment if they take it multiple times under similar conditions. If the student's scores fluctuate wildly, the assessment is likely to be unreliable. Most indicators that purport to measure student achievement are based on well-known, venerable assessments that have been demonstrated to have high levels of reliability; more caution and attention to reliability need to be paid when an assessment is newly developed for use in a specific indicator. All of the points made in this paragraph regarding test-retest reliability in the context of standardized assessments are just as applicable to survey questionnaires. The example of the indicator designed to measure the goals of high school guidance counseling programs illustrates how test-retest reliability is important in the case of survey questionnaires.

Several factors can influence the test-retest reliability of a standardized assessment or a survey questionnaire. We will not go into great detail about all of these factors, but two of the most visible and common determinants of reliability in sample surveys and standardized assessments are question wording and the environment in which the survey or assessment is administered. Questions that are posed in an unclear or confusing manner often induce low levels of test-retest reliability. Similarly, if the respondent takes an assessment or fills out a survey in an environment with many distractions, the resulting estimates are likely to have lower levels of reliability. Both developers and consumers of indicators should be especially cognizant of issues of question wording when creating and evaluating the quality of an indicator.

A second type of reliability that is relevant for the creation and evaluation of many indicators is interrater reliability. *Interrater reliability* is the degree of consensus between two or more individuals who are assessing the same concept or phenomenon. This dimension of reliability is important for indicators that require subjective assessments of a specific factor. Issues related to interrater reliability are most common when interviewers must classify individuals' responses during in-person or telephone interviews, but such issues can also arise when attempting to classify or categorize open-ended responses on survey questionnaires.

An example of the importance of interrater reliability can be found in an indicator report published by the National Center for Education Statistics that described the condition of school facilities (Planty & DeVoe, 2005). The estimates presented in the indicator report are based on a data collection instrument—a facilities checklist, to be specific—that was administered as part of the Education Longitudinal Study of 2002 (ELS:2002) (see NCES, 2002). As part of ELS:2002, interviewers traveled to schools and completed a checklist that contained items relevant to the conditions of school facilities. Specifically, the interviewers had to assess whether aspects of the school were in disrepair as well as the level of cleanliness within the school. While the checklist strived to include items that were entirely objective in nature, there was surely some subjectivity in the process of assessing the conditions of school facilities.[6] For example, interviewers were required to assess whether the floor and walls appeared clean and whether ceilings were in disrepair. There is undoubtedly a subjective element involved in making these assessments. However, the subjective nature of these assessments can be minimized through interviewer training and explicitly noting what should be considered when assessing the conditions of school facilities. This example is only one of many instances where interrater reliability may be an important component in creating and evaluating an indicator. Just as test-retest reliability should be considered when indicator estimates are constructed from a survey questionnaire or standardized assessment, issues associated with interrater reliability are relevant whenever multiple individuals are responsible for assessing the same concept or phenomenon.

The preceding paragraphs describe the concept of reliability and outline two specific types of reliability that are often applicable to the creation and evaluation of indicators. As was the case with validity, it can be difficult to determine the exact level of reliability in an indicator. However, there are some standard and well-accepted measures of reliability that consumers can look for when attempting to gauge the reliability of an indicator. For instance, when the estimates presented in an indicator rely on the subjective assessments of an interviewer or other indicators, consumers of the indicator can look for reports of interrater reliability. Often, the developers of an indicator will have multiple individuals assess an identical unit and report the interrater reliability statistic, which is the proportion of times that the individuals agreed in their assessments of the unit. Similarly, statistics can be calculated that measure the reliability of a standardized assessment or items on a survey questionnaire. We will not cover these measures in any detail here, but consumers should investigate such statistics if they encounter an indicator and question its reliability.

Validity and Reliability—Differences and Imperfections

The previous sections outlined the concepts of validity and reliability and highlighted their relevance to the creation and evaluation of indicators, especially with respect to issues of definition and measurement. In our descriptions of these complex and multidimensional concepts we employed a number of stylized examples to illustrate our points, but it is important to remember that an indicator is not simply valid or invalid. Similarly, an indicator cannot be easily classified as reliable or unreliable. As we described in Chapter 1, the concepts of reliability and validity can best be conceived as lying along a continuum; there are degrees of reliability and validity. Ideally, an indicator will have both a high degree of validity and a high degree of reliability. When this is the case, consumers of the indicator can be confident that the indicator is providing an accurate portrayal of the concept it purports to describe. Indicators with low levels of validity and reliability are generally suspect, and consumers must be cautious when interpreting these estimates. Indicators that fall in the middle—with either a high level of validity and a low level of reliability, or a high level of reliability and a low level of validity, or moderate levels of both—are the most difficult to judge. Depending on its purpose and intended use, an indicator with less than perfect validity and reliability may be just fine. Again, as we stressed earlier, it is the responsibility of the consumer to make an informed and educated judgment of the validity and reliability of the indicator, and thus decide whether it is suitable for the intended purpose of the consumer.

While we provided detailed descriptions of the concepts of validity and reliability above, it is useful to explicitly state how the two concepts differ and outline the consequences for an indicator if it lacks validity, reliability, or both. We stated earlier that validity is the extent to which the operational definition and measurement strategy employed in an indicator capture what it is attempting to capture. Expressed in the form of a question: How well does the operational definition line up with the conceptual definition? In contrast, reliability is the consistency of the operational definition. Regardless of whether the operational definition aligns with the conceptual definition, an indicator is reliable if the data collection instrument elicits the same, or similar, responses across multiple administrations.

So, given the differences between validity and reliability, what is the consequence of lacking either or both of these attributes? We first address the case of validity. If an indicator lacks validity it is not describing the concept it is intended to describe. In some cases, this can be a significant drawback; if the estimates presented in an indicator do not correspond to the conceptual definition, then the utility of the indicator may be limited. In other cases, however, relatively low levels of validity can be overcome as long as the consumer is aware of the shortcomings of the indicator and interprets the results accordingly. For example, consider our hypothetical example of the indicator that purported to measure statewide sixth-grade mathematics achievement, but the assessment used to measure achievement was only administered to students in four wealthy, suburban schools. In this case, the conceptual definition is not perfectly aligned with the operational definition and measurement strategy. As a result, the indicator does not have high external validity and thus is not entirely valid. However, the indicator may not be entirely useless. The estimates presented in the indicator likely provide a useful portrayal of sixth-grade mathematics achievement in wealthy, suburban schools. The consumer of the indicator can make use of this knowledge when attempting to understand statewide sixth-grade mathematics achievement.

If an indicator lacks validity it is not describing the concept it is attempting to describe. If an indicator lacks reliability, it may be describing the concept it purports to, but it may not be describing it accurately. Lacking reliability has the potential to be a very large problem. If consumers of an indicator cannot be confident that the estimates presented in an indicator accurately describe the concept in which they are interested, the indicator may be of little use. However, as was the case with validity, indicators without perfect levels of reliability may still possess utility. Consumers can compare the estimates presented in an indicator with other, potentially imperfect, indicators. If the indicators reach similar conclusions, then there may be reason to think that the results provide a fairly accurate representation of the concept of interest.

Overall, we want to stress that almost all indicators possess at least some imperfections with respect to validity and reliability. While the developers of indicators should strive to minimize these imperfections, it is incumbent upon the consumer of the indicator to recognize the imperfections that do exist and determine the precise manners in which the imperfections affect the utility and interpretation of the indicator. By describing the process of indicator creation and outlining a number of important issues that must be confronted and decisions that must be made during this process, this chapter has provided an introduction to a framework for making determinations about the utility and interpretation of indicators. Following chapters go further toward this goal and explicitly describe the sources of error in indicators, and provide a clear description of how such error can affect the value of indicators.

SUMMARY

This chapter began by emphasizing the importance of conceptualization, operationalization, and measurement. This emphasis was maintained throughout the chapter, which outlined each stage of the indicator creation process and described the issues that must be confronted and the decisions that must be made at each stage. To briefly recap the stages of the indicator creation process, indicators often emerge as a response to a perceived problem in the educational environment. After the decision has been made to create an indicator to monitor the status of the perceived problem, the first stage of the indicator creation process involves generating a precise conceptual definition of what the indicator will measure. This task can be more difficult than it may seem because there are often many intricacies and complicating factors that must be considered and addressed when developing a conceptual definition.

After a conceptual definition has been created, the task moves to developing an operational definition and measurement strategy. These two tasks are at the heart of the indicator creation process. While they can be conceived of as two separate tasks, in practice they often occur simultaneously; it would be foolish to operationally define a concept in a manner that is difficult or impossible to effectively measure. The process of operationally defining and measuring a concept can be effectively summarized by asking two questions: (1) Who will you ask? and (2) What will you ask?

These two questions are couched in the more technical terminology of question development and collection mode. The question of who to ask mainly involves determining whether the data used to create an indicator will be gleaned from administrative data or whether a sample survey will provide the requisite data. Each of these options has a unique composition of benefits and drawbacks that we described in solid detail throughout the chapter. The issue of what you will ask refers to the creation and composition of the data collection instrument. Will the concept be measured with a single item? Or is the concept multidimensional and multiple items will be required to provide an effective representation of the concept? Questions such as these will need to be addressed at this stage. Finally, the issue of how you will ask it requires consideration of the mode of data collection and question wording.

Throughout all of these stages, indicator developers will need to make a number of important decisions. This chapter emphasized that these decisions should be guided by the twin criteria of validity and reliability. Validity refers to the extent to which the operational definition and measurement strategy reflect the conceptual definition of an indicator. The concept consists of six dimensions—face validity, content validity, criterion validity, construct validity, external validity, and statistical validity—that are related, but conceptually distinct. Indicators should be evaluated along each of these dimensions to develop a sense of the overall validity of an indicator.

Reliability is the extent to which a given operational definition and measurement strategy yields consistent estimates of the concept it is designed to measure when the measurement is taken multiple times. We discussed two types of reliability—test-retest reliability and interrater reliability—that consumers of education indicators will often encounter. Assessments of both validity and reliability are subjective in nature, but consumers can rely on the definitions and descriptions described in this chapter to develop educated judgments.

Finally, this chapter outlined the consequences to an indicator when it lacks validity, reliability, or both attributes. Lacking these important characteristics will likely reduce the utility of an indicator, but it does not automatically render it completely useless. Depending upon its purpose and use, an indicator with low validity and reliability may serve some purposes just fine. Determining whether an indicator can be used for a specific goal is the responsibility of the consumer of the indicator.

CHAPTER 3

Sources of Information and Error

The individual source of the statistics may easily be the weakest link. Harold Cox tells a story of his life as a young man in India. He quoted some statistics to a Judge, an Englishman, and a very good fellow. His friend said, Cox, when you are a bit older, you will not quote Indian statistics with that assurance. The Government are very keen on amassing statistics—they collect them, add them, raise them to the nth power, take the cube root and prepare wonderful diagrams. But what you must never forget is that every one of those figures comes in the first instance from the *chowty dar* [village watchman], who just puts down what he damn pleases.

—*Josiah Stamp*

Now that we have described the stages of the indicator creation process and illustrated the important choices that must be made at each stage of the process, we need to look at the various sources of error that can bias the estimates presented in an indicator. The process from conceptualization through dissemination provides numerous opportunities for error to be introduced, and this chapter describes how error can be introduced into an indicator at each stage of the process. The discussion of the various sources of error is situated within a general framework for understanding an indicator's error structure. Understanding an estimate's error structure involves recognizing the different sources that might contribute to the estimate's overall error. All estimates have error, and identifying the significant sources is critical to understanding an indicator's value. The remainder of this introduction provides a cursory overview of the data collection, analysis, and presentation process and presents a brief summary of the major types of error that can influence the estimates presented in an indicator.

Possessing a comprehension of the processes of data collection, analysis, and presentation is vital to understanding how error can affect the estimates presented in an indicator; these processes provide a context for understanding error. We describe these processes in enough detail to allow for an understanding of the various types of error that may enter into indicators, which is our focus in this chapter.

The first stage of the data collection process involves conceptualization and measurement. Because this stage was described in sufficient detail in Chapter 2, we only briefly summarize it here: Conceptualization and measurement involve defining the topic the indicator is designed to describe, identifying an operational definition that balances considerations of validity and reliability with relevant constraints, and developing a measurement strategy for obtaining the data. The measurement strategy involves the construction of survey items and instruments that will be used to glean the desired information.

The second stage of the process involves the actual collection of all necessary data. Data collection requires the identification of the target population: To whom do we want the estimates presented in the indicator to be able to generalize? After identifying the target population, it must be decided whether data will be collected from every individual in the target population—universe data collection—or from a subset of the target population—sample data collection. Regardless of whether the data are collected from the full population or from only a sample of the population, it will need to be determined how the data will be collected. There are many options for collecting data, with some of the most common ones being in-person interviews, telephone interviews, mail surveys, and Internet surveys. Finally, decisions regarding timing will need to be made: When will the data be collected? Over how long of a time period? Questions such as these must be addressed during the process of collecting data.

After data have been collected, it must be processed. This involves checking many aspects of the data, including its format, its accuracy, and the amount of missing data. In short, it involves ensuring that the data are of acceptable quality to accomplish the purpose of the indicator. It is at this stage that analysts may implement procedures to mitigate problems associated with missing data and to review the data to ensure that the confidentiality of individuals from whom the data were collected will be protected.

Subsequent to the data being processed and converted into a useful format, attention turns to issues associated with analysis and display. At this stage of the indicator creation process, analysts will need to identify the metric they will use to convey the information to consumers, and create any tables or graphical depictions they will use to present the data. Furthermore, this stage involves determining the substantive significance of the data and information presented in the indicator. That is, analysts must determine whether the information is important for purposes of policy makers or educators. The following outline provides a clear and concise overview of the data collection, analysis, and presentation process:

1. Conceptualization and measurement: What kind of information are we after?
    a. Items
    b. Instrument
2. Data collection: How will we get that information?
    a. Target population and units
    b. Sample or universe collection
    c. Collection mode
    d. Timing
3. Processing: How do we construct the information into a useful form?
    a. Quality checks and edits
    b. Imputation
    c. Disclosure review
4. Analysis and display: How do we convey this information to the audience?
    a. Metrics
    b. Graphics
    c. Statistical testing
    d. Substantive importance

Different types of error can enter into an indicator at each of the stages of data collection, and the next few paragraphs provide a brief description of the main types of error that we discuss in this chapter. The first broad type of error that may affect indicators is sampling error. Sampling error arises because samples, by definition, only collect information from a subset of the population. Because not all individuals in the target population provide information, it is possible that the estimate constructed from the sample does not perfectly align with the true value in the population. Thankfully, samples are usually, but not always, chosen using a method—probability sampling—that allows for the amount of potential sampling error to be directly estimated. When samples are not chosen with a probability-based method, there is no way of estimating the potential amount of sampling error. While it may seem obvious, it is important to note that sampling error does not affect universe surveys.[1]

The second type of error that may be present in indicators is source error. The source is the individual or data source from which the information is collected. Information can be collected from individuals or through administrative or official records. For example, we can collect information from individual students by administering an assessment that will be used to describe student achievement, by administering a survey inquiring about how many times they were assaulted in order to describe school crime and safety, or by asking them whether they graduated from high school with a regular or honors diploma in order to portray high school graduation. Alternatively, we can rely on official records or administrative data to obtain information on grade point average, disciplinary history, and diploma credentials that can be used to describe the same concepts. In Chapter 2, we discussed how different sources of information have different sets of advantages and drawbacks. While source error is an important concept, it usually manifests itself through other types of error and so we do not present an explicit discussion of it; rather, we choose to address it in the context of the other types of errors discussed in this chapter.

The third potential source of bias in indicator estimates that we discuss in this chapter is nonsampling error. Nonsampling error is a catchall term, and refers to almost every other form of error besides sampling error and source error. Nonsampling error can occur during the collection, analysis, and presentation processes for both universe and sample survey collections. Specific types of error included under the umbrella of nonsampling error include coverage error, nonresponse error, measurement error, processing error, and dissemination and production error. These types of error can be difficult to identify and quantify but are probably the most significant concern for education indicators.

This chapter presents the major sources of error. By outlining the sources of information and identifying common types of errors associated with the collection, analysis, processing, and dissemination of estimates, the reader can have a better understanding of indicator quality. After going through the various components, we can then make a general assessment of the magnitude of error associated with a given estimate. It is quite possible that at one stage the error will be significant enough to render the indicator unfit for most purposes. In other cases the accumulation of error over multiple stages will result in both low reliability and validity.

WHY DOES ERROR EXIST?

Prior to describing the various sources of error that can affect the estimates presented in an indicator, it is useful to address why we need to be concerned with error at all. Can't we design and create an indicator that is able to be free of almost all error? It would clearly be preferable to have indicators of very high quality that are characterized by high validity and high reliability. However, such an ideal is seldom realized. Every data collection must be performed under constraints, and these constraints require decisions to be made that may result in lower data quality. That is, these decisions allow error to seep into the indicator. While there are many aspects of the data collection, analysis, and presentation process that relate to quality, the primary tensions generally occur between data quality and costs, respondent burden, and timeliness. These factors are interconnected and have complex relationships. Finding a proper balance will be dictated by the survey's purpose. As described in Chapter 2, quality has multiple dimensions, including high validity, high reliability, and relevance.

Every data collection must consider costs, and costs are related to the ability to devote time and resources to a particular collection. Trade-offs must inevitably be made between the ideal data collection process and, given funding constraints, the realistic data collection process. Issues of funding will enter into nearly every decision related to data collection, including the number of interviews that can be performed, the time spent with each respondent during the interview, and the mode of collection (in-person field interviews with computers are generally more expensive to conduct than self-administered survey via the mail or the Internet).

When funding constraints prevent the execution of the ideal data collection process, data analysts must acknowledge that with cheaper data collection vehicles generally comes lesser data quality. For example, mail surveys generally have much lower response rates than in-person interviews, a reality that can introduce both sampling and nonresponse error. In addition, respondents answering a survey administered by mail may be confused over questions or survey instructions and have no easy method for eliminating such confusion. A survey administered through an in-person or telephone interview allows for interviewer assistance. Furthermore, the type of data collection mode may present coverage problems. That is, a telephone interview will naturally miss households that do not have landline phones (including wireless-only households), but also those residents who screen their calls through answering services and machines (Blumberg & Luke, 2007). The trade-off between using a telephone mode versus an in-person mode is very likely to introduce sample bias. On the other hand, we also know that for some sensitive questions, respondents are more likely to answer these more accurately in the self-administered mail form compared to a face-to-face interview. Clearly, there are many trade-offs with quality and costs, and the data collection process must negotiate between all of these factors as they pertain to the survey's central purpose. Some types of trade-offs will introduce minor error, while others could seriously jeopardize the value and utility of the estimates presented in the indicator.

Related to costs is respondent burden. *Respondent burden* can be defined generally as the amount of time and resources a respondent needs to expend in order to complete a survey questionnaire. In school settings, burden also includes the number of students or teachers participating and the amount of physical space required for the execution of the data collection. For example, conducting a student assessment within a school may require a minimum of 2–3 hours of time with 30 or more students in a classroom or computer lab space. Students are pulled out of class, teachers or other staff may be needed to assist with logistics, and facilities are used for something other than their routine daily use. The longer or more complex a task, the more likely respondents will not participate or stop participating.

When analysts are making decisions related to respondent burden, they should recognize that clear, easy-to-answer, relevant questions are more likely to be answered. Long questionnaires, items that involve high cognitive demands by the respondent, questions that seem unnecessary, or those that are poorly worded are less likely to be answered correctly, if at all. Requests often go to schools for administrative records such as transcripts, disciplinary actions, and teacher records. Schools or districts that need to sort through multiple records or to reclassify existing records (for example, to place student GPAs on a different scale or to reclassify certain courses) to satisfy a survey's format will require considerable burden. Because of considerations of respondent burden, researchers will often have to trade off a questionnaire with multiple, in-depth questions that will provide high-quality information for a questionnaire that is concise, direct, and focused on the specific purpose.

Finally, timeliness is another factor that often needs to be traded off with data quality. There is a saying, "The perfect is the enemy of the good." Applied to the context of education indicators, this means that one can spend lots of resources and time to produce data and information that are of extremely high quality, but at some point they are good enough for the objective at hand. This is not to say that quality has been ignored, but rather that the estimates are accurate enough for the original purpose. We can spend hours interviewing respondents with thorough and detailed questionnaires, conduct rigorous data-quality checks and reviews, and assemble an exhaustive, detailed report on the topic of interest. However, the result may be a data system that is no longer timely or relevant to the questions at hand. Many large-scale national datasets take years to develop from initial conceptualization and instrument development, through the lengthy data collection and processing stages, to dissemination. It may be better to get out estimates that are of good quality now than to put out something of better quality later, when considering usability, value, and relevance.

These general types of trade-offs between cost, respondent burden, timeliness, and data quality, as well as more nuanced decisions, occur at every stage of the production process. Because the data collection processes always operate under constraints of costs, respondent burden, and timeliness, there are always trade-offs that must be made with data quality, and error is inevitable. This chapter provides a framework for understanding indicator error structure. The organization of this framework is as follows. First, we begin with a focus on the survey type (universe or sample) and then work through the major sources of error that can affect both survey types. Understanding survey type is a critical distinction because unlike universe collections, sample surveys are subject to sampling error. Finally, we identify five specific sources of nonsampling error that can occur throughout production process: coverage, nonresponse, measurement, processing, and production or dissemination errors. Again, remember that we will always have some amount and type of error. Error only becomes important when it has a significant effect on data quality. As we shall show, quantifying the amount of error is a difficult and subjective process.

The framework presented in this chapter is a systematic look at indicator quality. It is not a how-to for indicator construction. This is a slight, but important, distinction. We are not attempting to describe how a particular indicator should be created. That is determined by purpose, available resources, time, and so on. There are a number of excellent works that describe in detail the data collection process and errors related to these decisions (Biemer & Lyberg, 2003; Federal Committee on Statistical Methodology, 1978, 1988; Groves, 1989; Groves et al., 2009). Our goal is to provide a retrospective look at indicator quality as it was conceptualized, collected, measured, and analyzed. It is up to the reader to determine if, for a given purpose, the quality of an indicator is sufficient.

POPULATIONS VERSUS SAMPLES

A first step in the data collection process, beyond identifying the purpose and intentions of a particular collection, is to decide on our target population. A *target population* is simply the group of people we want to say something about. For example, the target population could consist of all teachers in the United States, all public school teachers, all public school secondary teachers, or even all public school secondary mathematics teachers. Once we establish the target population we address the very basic question: Should we attempt to collect information from every unit (person) in the target population of interest, or should we take a sample? This is the critical decision that serves as the starting point for understanding error.

Universe Surveys

Universe surveys collect information from all units within a target population. The primary advantage of universe surveys is that there is no need to account for sampling error, or the imprecision associated with estimating the value in a population using only a sample of the population. We get information from every unit in the population, so observed differences between groups are treated as real differences. There is no margin of error associated with the estimate. Further, universe surveys are often collected from existing administrative or official records (such as student transcripts, student disciplinary counts, or teacher payroll records) where costs can be minimal (or at least minimized) and where data quality for many items is relatively high.

However, the disadvantages of universe surveys are just as important to recognize. If the target population is large, collecting information from the universe can be very expensive and not very practical. Just imagine having to collect information from every public school student in the United States. There are approximately 50 million public school students scattered across the country. Collecting information from every student would require a tremendous amount of effort, time, and money. Further, timing becomes important because over the course of a year, the number of public students is somewhat dynamic. Students move in and out of the country, transfer between schools or districts, and drop out of school. The universe of public school students will vary depending upon the time of the year when data are collected. For example, many public students are not enrolled and are still in transition during the first week of any given school year. In Washington, D.C., 37,000 students were registered in the system's 127 schools on August 24, 2009, the first day of class. Three and a half weeks later, on September 15, the enrollment count stood at 44,397 (Turque, 2009). Official counts for many public schools occur in October when student enrollment has stabilized.

Universe surveys also result in slower collection times due to the number of contacts. Subsequently, due to the size and costs this will generally result in a limited number of items and less detailed data. Even when universe collections rely on administrative or official records, managing and processing thousands of records can be an arduous task. While costs and population sizes suggest that it is not always practical to collect universe surveys, a more important consideration is that it is not necessary for estimate reliability. A properly selected sample can provide very precise and reliable estimates for a fraction of the cost, time, and effort associated with a universe collection.

Sample Surveys

Given that the vast majority of education indicators are based on data collected from a sample of the target population, it is important that we provide the reader with an introduction to the properties of samples and the process of sampling. The first, and perhaps most obvious, question that arises when considering issues of data collection is: "Why sample? Why not take a universe collection?"

There are practical reasons for choosing a sample over a universe collection. First, and as described above, it can be very expensive and impractical to collect information from every person or unit in a particular population, especially if the population is large. Second, it is faster to collect a sample rather than a universe. Third, a properly selected sample can produce very accurate estimates of the true population value that would be obtained through a universe collection.

Samples also have disadvantages. The primary drawback associated with sampling is sampling error. *Sampling error* can be defined as "the variability that occurs by chance because a sample rather than an entire population was surveyed" (Kasprzyk & Giesbrecht, 2003). To illustrate the concept of sampling error, suppose we have a target population of 5,000 teachers, and we are interested in knowing their average salary. Within that target population there is a true population value of the average salary, and we could know the true average salary if we collected information from every teacher in the population. For the sake of this example, suppose that the average salary in the population is $50,000. However, for reasons of resource constraints, we can only collect information from a sample of 1,000 teachers. Within this sample, the average teacher salary is calculated to be $49,000. Now suppose we obtained enough resources to draw another sample of 1,000 teachers and calculate the mean salary. Within this sample, the average teacher salary is calculated to be $50,800. Both of these samples provide estimates of the average teacher salary, but because the estimates of teacher salary rely on different subsets of the full population they return similar but slightly different estimates. The difference between the true population value and the value estimated from a sample constitutes sampling error.

We quantify the size of the sampling error with a measure called the *standard error* or *margin of error*. A larger standard error is associated with less precision. The magnitude of the standard error is determined by three main factors: the number of individuals contained in the sample, the variation in the information collected from the respondents, and the method used to select the sample. In general, smaller sample sizes and more varied responses will lead to larger standard errors. Further, all else being equal, samples where the respondents are selected randomly have the lowest standard errors. However, many samples are not selected randomly. Samples that are not selected randomly are referred to as *complex samples* and are less efficient, meaning that they result in higher standard errors. As a result, we can be less confident in the precision of the estimates. Having a general understanding as to how samples are selected is important to understanding the estimate's reliability and validity. So if we are to sample, there are two factors we must be aware of—representativeness and reliability.

The Sampling Process

We take samples every day. In fact, many everyday activities can be thought of as sampling. We sample music groups by listening to songs on the radio; we sample vacation destinations when we spend a weekend at a particular beach resort; we sample a restaurant when we choose a few items off the menu; we sample colors when we test the look of two or three new paint colors for the living room wall. Each sample is a subset of the whole. A critical factor in the sampling process involves whether the sample you observe or experience is *representative* of the larger population as a whole. So when you hear a song on the radio by a particular music group, the question is whether the rest of the songs on the artist's album will have the same qualities.

The second element is *reliability*. As mentioned in Chapter 2, there are two general dimensions of reliability. The first dimension involves consistency and the ability to get the same result, under the same conditions, time after time. We often refer to a reliable worker as someone who shows up on time each day and produces consistent results each day. In the context of education indicators, reliability may refer to a student assessment that, when given multiple times under the same set of conditions, produces scores that are similar. We would not want to use a test that classifies a student as a low performer one day and then a high performer the next. Student knowledge and academic ability do not fluctuate to that degree on a day-to-day, or even a year-to-year, basis.

The second dimension of reliability addresses sampling precision. In this dimension, reliability is quantitatively measured by the standard error and can be thought of as the confidence you have that the statistical estimates are reflective of the true estimate. Larger standard errors are less reliable. The key to understanding this type of precision is to understand how samples are selected.

Sampling basics

Sampling is the process of selecting observations. As described earlier, samples are drawn when it is not possible or preferable to collect all observations within a population. Statistically, we know that it is not necessary to collect information from all units in a population if we use probability theory to design our collection. The logic of probability sampling allows us to make generalizations from observed cases to the whole group. That is, if we make some assumptions about the larger population, we can select a sample, and estimates from that sample will reflect the true value in the population, with some margin of error. We call the error associated with taking a sample versus collecting information from the entire population sampling error. Sampling error can be reflected in the standard error of the estimate. The smaller the standard error, the more reliable the estimate. The size of the standard error is driven in part by the number of units in the sample chosen (or more directly the effective sample size) and the heterogeneity or variability in the sample responses. Very simply, the closer the sample size is to the actual population size, the more confident you are in your estimate.

Similarly, the less variability in how respondents answer a particular question, the more confident you are that the estimate reflects the true value. So probability sampling tends to produce reliable and valid estimates, estimates with precision that reflect the larger population. There are many probability-based sampling strategies. Two general techniques commonly used represent the general spectrum: simple random and complex.

The first task in developing and drawing a sample involves establishing the sampling frame. Establishing the sampling frame requires identifying the population of interest and developing a list of potential units from which you will select your sample; this list is the *sampling frame*. For example, within a district a superintendent may have an interest in how teachers perceive the work environment. Is it safe, supportive, and clean? Instead of collecting information from all teachers within the district, the superintendent could select a sample of teachers from a list of all teachers that was generated from administrative records or payroll. In a *simple random sample* (SRS), which is the most basic type of sampling procedure, every teacher has an equal chance of being selected into the sample. This allows for the avoidance of biases and allows for the construction of accurate population estimates. In theory, the sample will represent the larger population of teachers.

Selecting a simple random sample is a relatively straightforward exercise, but it has a number of limitations. It may be that the sample selection process does not produce a random selection and by chance you have a biased sample. For example, by chance you might end up with all female teachers and no males. To ensure proper levels of important, policy-relevant groups, other sampling strategies are employed, which are referred to as complex samples. Most education indicators rely on data collected through complex samples.

Complex samples

Complex sampling strategies are employed when simple random samples are not possible or efficient. The two most common types of complex sampling strategies are referred to as cluster sampling and stratified samples. Cluster sampling generally occurs in multiple stages, and the procedure can best be illustrated by the following example. Suppose that we define our target population as all students attending elementary or secondary school in the United States. Unfortunately, there is no comprehensive list of every student attending elementary or secondary school in the United States that could serve as our sampling frame. There does, however, exist a comprehensive list of all elementary and secondary schools in the country. We can use this list as our sampling frame. In the first stage of cluster sampling we select a sample of schools from the sampling frame. Then, we would go to each school that was selected to be in the sample and request a list of all students enrolled in the school. In the second stage of the cluster sample, we then select a sample of students from the enrollment lists provided by each school. So, in general, cluster sampling involves selecting a sample of units from an existing sampling frame and then selecting a sample of individuals from within those units.

The benefits of cluster sampling stem from issues of cost and sampling frames. With respect to sampling frames, for many target populations there is often no readily available list of all members in the population. For example, there are no comprehensive lists of students, teachers, guidance counselors, or many other potential units of interest. As a result, researchers must identify other methods of sampling these populations. Luckily, each of these populations are all clustered within schools and there is a list of every elementary and secondary school in the country that can serve as the sampling frame. By first selecting a group of schools from the sampling frame and then selecting individuals from the rosters provided by the schools, we can generate a sample that is representative of the target population. This type of sampling is referred to as a *two-stage cluster design;* first schools are sampled and then individuals within schools. Most nationally representative surveys in education employ two-stage cluster designs where, in the first stage, a sample of schools is selected from a school universe file. Then, in the second stage, individuals are sampled from the schools selected in the first stage. Similar issues arise in many other organizational contexts as well. For example, identifying a comprehensive list of police officers, nurses, corporate workers, or prisoners to serve as the sampling frame is often impossible. This problem is solved by using a cluster design where police stations, hospitals, corporations, or prisons are sampled in the first stage and individuals within these units are sampled in the second stage. Cluster designs are often used to sample the general public as well. First, a survey may sample counties, neighborhoods, or households and then sample individuals within these units.

The other advantage to a cluster design relates to costs. A simple example will make it clear. If we are to select 40 students, it is far more efficient to select these 40 students from a single school than to randomly select 40 students from across the country. The costs associated with travel time, set-up, selection, and collection are minimized by clustering sample members. However, this data collection efficiency comes at a cost to statistical efficiency. It may be obvious from the prior example, but 40 students selected from one school will be more alike in their responses than 40 students randomly selected across the nation. As a result, we need to adjust our standard error to account for the fact that students will be more alike in their responses. We will not get into the statistical procedures that are used to make such adjustments, but suffice it to say that the adjustments increase the size of our standard error and thus make our estimates less precise.

Another common complex sampling technique is stratification. Stratification involves selecting units independently within predefined subgroups of interest. *Stratification* helps to ensure adequate sample sizes for subgroups that are important or policy-relevant. Because larger sample sizes decrease an estimate's standard error and thus increase precision and reliability, we are able to construct better estimates for subgroups when stratification techniques are employed. Prior to sampling, all potential sample members are sorted by a set of available policy-relevant variables. For national school samples, this may include the school's type (elementary, secondary, combined), sector (public, private), locale (rural, suburban, city), and school size. Once the population is sorted and sample sizes are determined for each subgroup, or stratum,[3] the sample is selected. Stratification has the tendency to improve statistical efficiency by decreasing the size of the standard errors and improving reliability.

Almost every large-scale national survey employs some combination of clustering and stratification. The combined impact of these design features on the sample precision and efficiency is captured in a term called the *design effect*. The design effect tells us how the complex sampling strategies (used to improve costs, to address a lack of proper sampling frame, to ensure adequate sample sizes for precision) affect an estimate's precision, relative to a simple random sample. Samples with large design effects are less precise or reliable than those with smaller design effects.

Both SRS and complex samples are based on probability theory and drawn from known sampling frames. However, it is quite common to come across non-probability-based sample surveys. For example, *convenience samples* do not use information about the population to select sample members, but collect information from sample members in a population based on easy availability, or convenience. While this might control costs and increase timeliness, there is no way to know if the sample generalizes to the larger population. Therefore, any estimate will be suspicious and assumed to lack an adequate level of external validity.

WEIGHTING SAMPLES

Because samples are a subset of the population, the information from each sample member is often "inflated" by some factor in order to produce accurate population estimates. This inflation is generally accomplished through the use of weights. *Weights* are the adjustment factors needed to produce these population estimates from samples. When complex sampling proce-dures are used, the raw sample often consists of individuals who are not fully representative of the target population. Furthermore, issues of unit nonresponse—some groups refuse to participate at different rates than oth-ers—can complicate the construction of population estimates. Not account-ing for these factors can lead to biased estimates and departures from the true population values. Weighting the sample can correct for these issues.

In practical terms, a weight is simply a number by which each case in the sample is multiplied. The number used to multiply each sample case is equivalent to the number of other members in the population that the sample member represents. A simple exercise will help to illustrate the con-cept of weights. Imagine a population of 100 students. We take a random sample of 10 students from the population of 100. Each sample member represents 10 other students, all else being equal, so the weighting factor or weight is 10. If we had taken a sample of 20 members from this population the weight would be 5. Each sample member selected would represent 5 other students in the population. However, we know that for many national studies a complex sample is employed and there is often a significant level of unit nonresponse.[4] We must account for this nonresponse when calculating our weights.

As an example, the Education Longitudinal Study of 2002, or ELS:2002 (NCES, 2002) examines the educational pathways and attainment of the 2002 sophomore class. The Education Longitudinal Study of 2002 over-samples Asian students and private school students (again, to be sure we have enough sample members in the population for reliable estimates). It is also a sample with unit nonresponse (some students did not want to participate). Since we have both oversampling and nonresponse, weights are developed to account for the disproportionate representation of cer-tain groups in the sample. Table 3.1 shows the unweighted and weighted counts and percent distributions for each race or ethnic group. There are two problems with the unweighted data. First, the total for the unweight-ed sample is only 13,180 students. We know that this count is too low to be the entire population of sophomore students in 2002; it represents only those students who were sampled. However, once we weight the es-timates we get the true population size, which is approximately 2.9 mil-lion students. So it is very important to weight the sample when you are producing estimates for the number of graduates, dropouts, students with disabilities, and so on. If weights are not employed, the estimated counts will be severely underestimated.

This first problem is probably obvious to most readers. Less obvious is the second problem related to percentages and population distributions.

Table 3.1. Unweighted and weighted counts and percentages for the 2002 sophomore cohort of the Education Longitudinal Study of 2002

	Unweighted		Weighted	
Race/ethnicity	Count	Percent	Count	Percent
American Indian/Alaska Native, non-Hispanic	100	0.8	27,733	0.9
Asian, Hawaii/Pacific Islander, non-Hispanic	1,350	10.3	129,257	4.4
Black or African American, non-Hispanic	1,640	12.4	390,635	13.3
Hispanic, no race specified	800	6.0	191,295	6.5
Hispanic, race specified	980	7.5	238,739	8.2
White, non-Hispanic	7,720	58.6	1,834,490	62.7
Total	**13,180**	**100.0**	**2,927,562**	**100.0**

Source. U.S. Department of Education, National Center for Education Statistics, Education Longitudinal Study of 2002 (ELS:2002), "Base year, 2002," special tabulations by author.

We see in the unweighted column that Asians make up about 10.3% of the sample. This is much too high, but expected because we oversampled these students given our concern about having adequate sample sizes (that is, we selected these students at higher rates than other race groups). Once we weight the cases we produce the correct point estimates for percentages, with Asians making up just 4.4% of the student population for this cohort. In fact, we see slight adjustments to all groups since the weight will capture oversampling, unit nonresponse, and other features of the sample design and post-collection adjustments. So in most cases, samples should be weighted to produce accurate point estimates. Failure to properly weight a sample could result in indicators presenting biased estimates.

A LESSON IN WEIGHTING: TEENAGE DRINKING

Researchers released a study claiming that underage drinkers (ages 12–20) accounted for 25% of all drinking in the United States. This statistic was widely reported, but also incorrect. The researchers did not account for the disproportionate number of teenagers in the sample due to oversampling and used unweighted estimates. Teenagers made up 40% of the sample, but make up less than 20% of the population. Therefore, the unweighted estimates for teenage drinking were biased upward and much too high. The correct estimate for underage drinking was less than half of the original and closer to 11%. Not recognizing the attributes of the sample design led to biased estimates (Lewin, 2002).

NONSAMPLING ERROR

Nonsampling errors can be defined as the larger set of errors that can occur during the indicator creation process regardless of whether the indicator is based on a universe or sample survey collection. These sources include coverage error, nonresponse error, measurement error, processing error, and dissemination and production error. These types of error are more difficult to identify and quantify, but probably represent the most significant concern for education statistics.

Coverage Error

Coverage error is the error in the estimate resulting from a failure to include some units in the estimate that should be included (undercoverage error) and failure to exclude units that should not be included or are included multiple times (overcoverage). Coverage error can occur in both universe and sample surveys. The primary source of coverage error in both survey types is the quality of the sampling frame. If the sampling frame is out of date or contains unreliable information, the probability of missing units or double counting units is great. For example, conducting a teacher salary survey relying on teacher rosters that were constructed 1–2 years earlier will probably lead to lots of bad information given the level of teacher mobility. Many new teachers will be missed. Another issue concerns the completeness of the sampling frame or selection list with respect to the actual target population. For example, a common concern for estimates of educational attainment concerns the ability of a telephone or household survey to capture every person properly. Telephone surveys will miss households that rely exclusively on wireless phones. Household surveys typically miss persons who are institutionalized or are part of the military. For example, estimates of educational attainment collected from the Current Population Survey (U.S. Census Bureau, n.d.) do not capture persons who are incarcerated at the time of the survey. This estimate is bound to overestimate the educational attainment of males given their relatively high incarceration rate and the fact that incarcerated individuals tend to have lower education levels.

A Lesson in Coverage Error: Household Phone Surveys

One common mode of data collection is the telephone survey. It has many advantages, including the centralizing of data collection operations and the ability to collect information quickly with real-time data entry. However, there are a number of serious disadvantages. Beyond concerns about households screening calls and refusing to participate if contacted, there has been a tremendous growth in wireless-only households. Research has shown significant increases in the numbers of individuals living in wireless-only households and wireless households tend to be very different than landline households (Blumberg & Luke, 2009). About 18% of all adults, or 41 million, live in wireless-only households and this percentage has been steadily increasing. These households tend to be disproportionately young, unrelated roommates, male, low-income, and Hispanic. The decrease in traditional landline phone service has led to growing concern about coverage problems with telephone surveys. It becomes apparent that because of the significant coverage error associated with the landline telephone data collection mode, there is a serious chance of biased results. Other work by Blumberg and Luke (2007) provides additional evidence that landline-only phone surveys lead to bias estimates for a variety of measures.

Selection Bias

Closely related to coverage error is the concept of selection bias. *Selection bias* occurs when specific parts of a targeted population are selected while others are left out of the survey collection. This can be a product of poor coverage with a sampling frame or significant unit nonresponse. Other instances of selection bias are intentional, such as when schools respond to high-stakes testing by reshaping the testing population.

Figlio (2006) examined the disciplinary practices of school officials and found that schools employ selective punishment in an apparent attempt to shape the testing pool. Given the high stakes associated with state-mandated test scores, some schools apparently target students with a record of low performance with longer suspension periods, which subsequently prevents them from participating on tests. Figlio found that lower-performing students were more likely to be suspended at test time and for longer periods than their higher-performing classmates, even for the same infraction. Figlio compared suspension rates of students involved in over 41,000 incidents in which two students were suspended and when test scores for both students were available. Schools tended to assign longer punishments to low-performing students than to high-performing students throughout the year, but this gap increased substantially during the testing period. That is, students with the lowest scores in reading and mathematics on the state test were suspended for more days compared to students who performed better on the test. Figlio also investigated other ways schools reshape the testing pool in an attempt to inflate school test score indicators. Florida schools tend to reclassify lower-performing students as disabled at significantly higher rates during the testing process (Figlio & Getzler, 2006). These types of responses to high-stakes testing and indicators are not uncommon.

Nonresponse Error

Nonresponse error occurs when individuals who have been selected to be sampled are missing from data that have been collected, usually because they refuse to participate. The response rate is the metric used to capture the potential size of this error and, like coverage rates, as a measure of survey quality. Surveys with higher response rates are seen as more desirable because it is assumed that when response rates are higher, the estimate constructed from the sample will better reflect the true population value.

For example, a survey of parents might result in a response rate of 95%, 85%, 50%, or any other level. A 95% response rate is excellent, and the small proportion of non-responders suggests that nonresponse bias is unlikely to play a role in an indicator. At a response rate of 85%, however, the threat of bias becomes more real (Seastrom, 2002). It is generally assumed that once you get to a response rate in the 85% range, it is likely that non-respondents are substantively different than respondents. In addition, when response rates drop down to this range, the proportion of nonrespondents can become large enough to affect the estimates presented in the indicator. Indeed, this is the view taken by NCES and other notable disseminators of education indicators.

Despite this conventional wisdom, the research examining the relationship between response rates and the bias of an estimate is mixed. In reality, nonresponse bias is not directly related to the response rate per se but rather to innate differences between responders and nonresponders (Groves, 2006). Of course, having a response rate very close to 100% is ideal and a minimum number of nonresponders is likely to have a minimal impact on estimates.

Many surveys are conducted over time, and a concern that is specific to these types of surveys is response rates that change over time. In general, higher response rates are desirable. However, if the response rates for the early years of a survey are substantially different from the response rates for later years of the survey, then it is not clear that the estimates across years are comparable. The potential incomparability stems from the fact that the variable response rates may result in the survey estimates representing different underlying populations. Of course, we know that the composition of populations changes over time and we would want a survey to reflect such changes. However, it is difficult to know whether the composition of the true population has changed over time; one purpose of a survey is to indicate whether such changes have occurred. Varying response rates complicate this purpose because it is difficult to know whether any observed changes in estimates over time are attributable to changes in the true population or only to changes in the "responding" population. A similar problem afflicts surveys that experience significant declines in participation rates. As nonresponse rates increase over the years, it is quite likely that any changes in the actual estimates will be a product, in part, of the changing portion of the participation population.

While unit nonresponse is important, item nonresponse rates are equally important. Item nonresponse or more generally "item missingness" is caused when a respondent doesn't answer a specific question. They may refuse to provide an answer (often this is the case with sensitive questions related to income, drug use, victimizations, or sexual activity), skip it (longer or more detailed questions may increase burden), simply miss it, or, on timed interviews, just not get to it. As with unit nonresponse, item nonresponse can introduce bias if the responders are significantly different from the nonresponders.

A Lesson in Nonresponse Error: Student Volunteer Behavior

Volunteer service is a critical component of our society, and as a result estimating the number of volunteers and the trends in volunteering behaviors over time is of interest to many. Abraham, Helms, and Presser (2009) examined annual estimates of volunteering and found estimates ranging from 28% in the Current Population Survey (CPS) to 39% in the National Household Education Survey (NHES) to a high of almost 50% in the Independent Sector Survey. Further, one indicator shows that volunteering rates have almost doubled between 1977 and 1991.

The authors note, however, that one significant source of difference between these estimates and within the trend survey over time is varying response rates. For example, the CPS survey had an 82% response rate compared with a 59% response rate for NHES. The authors examined the relationship between volunteering estimates and response rates and found an inverse relationship: the higher the response rate the lower the volunteering rate. Their hypothesis to explain this relationship was that survey participation is similar to volunteering, and those people who are more apt to volunteer are more apt to respond to surveys. They explored this hypothesis further and confirm that the greater propensity of those who do volunteer work to respond to surveys leads to estimates of volunteering that are too high. As a result, the increase in the volunteering rate over time may be a product of declining response rates.[5] The bias suggests that the survey estimates have lower external validity and the results are not likely to generalize to the larger population.

This type of nonresponse bias is likely to apply to other survey estimates of volunteering and other prosocial behaviors. For example, there are a number of studies that examine student engagement. One such study is the National Survey of Student Engagement (NSSE), which surveys freshmen and seniors to find out how engaged they are in academic and social activities (National

Survey, 2009a). The average institutional response rate for this study was 36% with a student response rate of 31% (National Survey, 2009b). It is quite likely that the types of students responding to this survey are the ones who are more likely to be "engaged." Subsequently, estimates about the level and types of engagement will be biased. It is also a concern that increases in institutional participation rates may lead to biased trend lines. The number of participating institutions has increased from 276 schools in 2000 to 610 in 2007, while student response rates have declined slightly.

Measurement Error

Measurement error can be defined as the difference between the observed value of a variable and the true population value (Kasprzyk & Giesbrecht, 2003). Measurement error is caused by inaccuracies in the responses collected from survey instruments due to interviewers, respondents, questionnaires, or data collection modes. Measurement errors are difficult to identify and quantify. Most often these types of errors are diagnosed through experimentation. For example, one can look at the effect of data collection modes by conducting the same survey by phone or in person. Any difference would be attributed to a mode effect. However, it's often difficult to know which estimate is the correct estimate. If the telephone interviews produced systematically higher estimates compared to the in-person interviews, a researcher must still make a decision about over- and underreporting errors. This is most often done in relation to the study's purpose and topic. While these types of errors are not easy to get a handle on and most data collection is designed to avoid obvious measurement errors, it is still of importance to recognize potential data limitations in any system.

Interviewers can affect survey responses. There are a number of studies that show that different interviewers can produce different estimates within the same data collection system. For example, unlike a mailed-out, self-administered survey, skilled interviewers can increase participation and assist respondents through the questionnaire. Interviewer characteristics may interact with respondent characteristics during the interview process. For example, a male respondent may respond differently to a female interviewer than to a male interviewer. The differences may be attributed to social desirability, which is the tendency for respondents to reply to questions in a way that will be viewed as socially acceptable. This is especially problematic with surveys containing sensitive questions about sexual behaviors, drug use, or victimization. Other items such as income, political preferences, and positions on contentious issues may be affected by the interview process. The interviewer-respondent interaction can be more pronounced when the interview is in person versus over the phone. Respondents may be less likely to respond to sensitive questions with an in-person, face-to-face interview.

The characteristics of the respondents will also affect measurement error. Respondent comprehension, retrieval ability, and communication are vital for producing accurate responses. If respondents have trouble remembering events, have distorted or selective memories, or simply don't understand what is being asked, estimates will likely be biased. In many surveys one respondent will answer for the entire household. Ideally this should be the person most knowledgeable about the topic. For example, the primary care-giver is usually the preferred respondent for questions that relate to the type and level of educational preparation experienced by the children in the household. It is assumed that the person who cares for the child on a daily basis will have a better understanding and recollection for these types of questions.

The impact of questionnaire and item design has been extensively re-searched (Sudman, Bradburn, & Schwarz, 1996). There are a host of poten-tial errors associated with the construction of questionnaires. Faulty ques-tions and wording (e.g., questions that are leading the respondent to answer a certain way or questions that are incorrect) will generate inaccurate es-timates. Long and complex questions and wording will increase respon-dent burden and confuse respondents. Incomplete or redundant response categories will force respondents to select a wrong answer. In some cases, respondents may be faced with response categories that do not match their situation. For example, a survey on student coursework and performance may ask a student for a grade point average on a scale from 0–4. However, school grading systems vary, with some adopting a 5-point letter system (A–F), others a 13-point letter system (A–F with pluses and minuses), oth-ers with numeric systems ranging from 0–4 to 0–242, and some schools do not use grades. Many schools allow for GPAs to exceed the normal range when college-level work is taken (e.g., Advanced Placement courses). Some schools calculate both a total and an academic GPA that focuses only on core classes and not electives, physical education, or credits in extracur-ricular courses. The GPA item requires students to convert their school's scale into the 0–4 metric. Students often do not know how to convert their GPA into the 0–4 metric so they generally just take their best guess, which may or may not be close to the true answer. The range of issues related to questionnaire development and item construction are too many to discuss here. However, in general, questions perform best when they are clearly written, have conceptual clarity, are short, and reflect recent events. Once respondent burden is increased, either through demands on recall, cognitive challenges, or confusing items, error can be significant.

Of course, no study is able to eliminate measurement error. Compro-mises are made routinely to minimize costs and time, but these compromises must be gauged against reductions in data quality.

Measurement error may occur when the respondent does not understand the question or when the response categories are not properly defined. The Current Population Survey (CPS) and Decennial Census are used to produce national estimates on educational attainment. However, there is some ambiguity in how respondents self-classify their highest level of attainment. Black, Sanders, and Taylor (2003) examined the measurement error in reporting higher education levels by comparing the Decennial Census to a more detailed and presumably more accurate follow-up survey, the National Survey of College Graduates (NSCG). The longer, more detailed NSCG was able to do a better job classifying student attainment due to its more detailed questioning compared to the limited Census/CPS single-question approach. Since these were the same sample members responding to two different surveys, measurement error could be identified.

The authors found substantial error in reporting higher educational attainment in the CPS, resulting in "degree creep," and these errors varied widely by demographic goups. That is, many respondents overreported their educational attainment on the Census/CPS question when compared to the NSCG. Only 91% of respondents who reported a BA degree in the Census also reported having a BA degree in the NSCG. Similar, but higher, mismatch rates were found for master's and doctoral degrees, but the most striking finding was for professional degrees (e.g., JD, MD, DDS, and so on): Only 66% of the respondents who reported a professional degree in the Census/CPS reported having a professional degree in the NSCG and 17% had no college degree at all. The authors estimate that well over half of women who reported having a professional degree did not have one. Upon further investigation, a substantial portion of the misreported data appear to be related to language problems or misunderstanding of the classification of degrees. Many respondents had earned continuing education or certificates in specialized fields such as hairdressing, cosmetology, health fields, and health technicians. It is likely that they interpreted these certificates as being "professional degrees." Such errors lead to significant underestimations of the labor market returns for higher education, especially for women.

Processing and Adjustment Error

Processing error is error introduced after the data are collected and are cleaned prior to analysis. *Cleaning the data* refers to putting the information into readable forms using some type of computer program, which involves data entry, coding verbatim or open-ended questions, and handling missing items, outliers, and anomalies. Errors can occur during the process of cleaning the data, but rarely are they systematic and exert a substantial bias on estimates.

Analysis and Dissemination Errors

The errors described above can occur in both universe and sample data collections. However, the potential for the introduction of error does not disappear when all the data have been collected. The potential for distortion and misunderstanding can also occur during the analysis and dissemination phases of indicator creation. As the next chapter will describe in greater detail, choosing the most appropriate metrics, analytical approach, comparisons, and visual displays (graphs and tables) is critical to communicating the findings of an indicator. Inappropriate metrics, the presentation of selective findings or years, the use of graphics with poorly chosen scales, and the choice of unfair comparison groups can only lead to confusion and misinterpretation.

A Lesson in Analysis and Dissemination: SAT Scores

To illustrate how error can occur during the analysis and dissemination phase, let's look at an example of a comparison of SAT scores across states. In 1984, the Secretary of Education released a state-by-state comparison of a variety of education performance, resource, and population variables, known as the "Wall Chart" (Wainer, Holland, Swinton, & Weng, 1985). As might be expected, these performance comparisons resulted in a substantial amount of publicity (Powell & Steelman, 1996). One variable in particular that was the subject of intense media attention was the mean college admissions test scores by states, which were presented as a measure of the effectiveness of a state's educational system. While the Department of Education cautioned that these test scores should be viewed in conjunction with the other measures shown on the chart, the comparison of unadjusted state SAT scores was too good to pass up for many media and policy outlets. Unfortunately, comparing SAT scores among states suffers from at least one critical problem: differential participation rates (Powell & Steelman, 1984; Wainer et al., 1985). Powell and Steelman (1996) note that SAT participation rates in 1993 ranged from a low of 4% in Utah and Mississippi to a high of 88% in Connecticut.[9] Furthermore, they find 80% of the difference in SAT scores across states was due to these varying participation rates. They explain:

> The reason is simple. In states where the percentage of students taking the SAT is high, the proportion of less motivated or low-achieving students tak-

ing the test is also high, thus yielding a lower average state SAT score than in those states where the percentage of students taking the exam is low. (Powell & Steelman, p. 32)

As in 1993, similar disparities in admission test participation rates exist today. Some states have called for the use of adjusted SAT scores based on student demographic variables and exam participation rates (Powell & Steelman, 1996; Wainer, 1990; Wainer et al., 1985). Others have extended the use of adjustments to other indicators (e.g., graduation rates) in an effort to make fair comparisons between groups (Salganik, 1994). The lesson that can be gleaned from this example is that care needs to be taken during the process of analysis and dissemination to ensure that the information presented in an indicator is not subject to distortion or misinterpretation.

SUMMARY

All indicators provide estimates of a true population value. Each estimate has error, and understanding the error structure is critical to understanding the substantive value of any indicator. While it is impossible to know all sources of error associated with an indicator, there are some fundamental questions any researcher can ask to evaluate the error structure. A general series of questions provides a framework.

FRAMEWORK FOR UNDERSTANDING INDICATOR ERROR STRUCTURE

1. Is the indicator based on data from a sample? If yes, are any of the following concerns relevant?
   a. Was the sample selected using probability-based methods? If not, external validity is questionable.
   b. Do standard errors or margins of error accompany the estimates presented in an indicator? If not, the reliability or precision of the estimates is not clear.
      i.   If standard errors are presented, are they relatively small? If not, the estimates may lack precision and reliability.
   c. Are the estimates weighted properly to produce population estimates? If not, the estimates will be biased and incorrect.

2. Regardless of whether the indicator is based on data from a sample or universe collection, are any of the following concerns relevant?

a. Does the sampling frame fully cover the target population?   If not, coverage error exists and the estimates in the indicator may not be generalizable to the target population.

b. What are the response rates at the unit and item levels? Low response rates at either level have the potential to introduce bias into the estimates presented in the indicator.

    i.   If the survey is conducted over time, have response rates changed? If so, the comparability of the estimates is unclear.

c. Is the indicator subject to measurement error?

    i.   Does the indicator describe a concept or subject of a sensitive or personal nature? If so, people might have misreported information, if they elected to report information at all.

    ii.   Are there any potential mode effects? The consumer should consider how the mode of data collection might affect estimates presented in the indicator.

    iii.   Are there any potential interviewer effects? The consumer should consider how interactions between respondents and interviewers might affect estimates presented in the indicator.

    iv.   Are there any potential respondent effects? The consumer should consider how the characteristics of the respondents might affect estimates presented in the indicator.

    v.   Were the survey items clear and concise? A lack of clarity or concision has the potential to introduce measurement error.

d. Were the data processed and cleaned in an accurate and systematic manner? If not, processing error has the potential to be introduced.

e. Were the data analyzed and presented in the most appropriate manner? Failure to do so could result in the indicator presenting a distorted or misleading picture of the concept it intends to describe.

CHAPTER 4

Statistics and Data Presentation

A drunk is searching on his hands and knees underneath a street lamp when a friend spots him and asks what he is doing. "Looking for my keys," is the reply. The friend gets down on his hands and knees to join the search. After half an hour the friend asks, "Are you sure you dropped them here?" "No," the drunk says, "I dropped them over there in those bushes," motioning to a spot some distance away. "Then why are you searching here?" the friend asks. "The light is better over here," the drunk replies.

—*Unknown*

Figures don't lie, but liars figure.

—*Mark Twain*

The previous chapters highlighted and described the importance of definitions, measurement, and data collection. Decisions made during these stages of indicator creation undoubtedly play a large role in shaping the quality of an indicator. However, making optimal decisions at these stages of the indicator creation process does not guarantee that an indicator will be of high quality. Indeed, even indicators that have well-designed definitions and well-implemented measurement strategies and data collection procedures can have relatively little value if the indicator presents the data or information in a confusing or ineffective manner. The methods that are used to present and describe the data are just as important as the stages of definition, measurement, and data collection. If used well, statistics and statistically based graphics can present complex information in a clear and convincing manner. However, if used ineffectively, they can also distort and obscure important information that may be contained in an indicator. This chapter will provide readers with a toolkit for assessing the methods used to present information in indicators.

We begin by describing basic statistical concepts and measures that are used in the presentation and interpretation of education indicators. Specifically, we discuss common metrics (counts, percentages, rates, percentiles, rankings), measures of central tendency (mean, median, mode), and measures of dispersion (range, variance, standard deviation, coefficient of variation). In the next section we present a slightly more advanced discussion of standard errors, weights, and statistical testing. We follow up the introduction to these concepts with a discussion of substantive significance and effect sizes. While we discuss all of these concepts in several contexts, special attention is given to student assessments and test scores.

In a final section we focus briefly on data presentation. Specifically, we discuss the presentation of data in tables and charts and outline the important elements to consider during this process, with consideration of the various graphical options that are available and commonly used to present information in indicators.

STATISTICAL CONCEPTS AND MEASURES

After the tasks associated with developing a definition, outlining a measurement strategy, and implementing a data collection plan have been completed, attention turns to determining the best metric for presenting the information that the indicator is designed to convey. There are usually several available options for presenting data and information in an indicator, and it is the responsibility of the creator of the indicator to settle on the format that is appropriate for the situation at hand. In essence, the developer needs to determine which metric would best convey the information in a clear and meaningful manner.

We describe these groups of metrics in this section. First, there are a few common metrics that the majority of all indicators use to convey information: counts and statistics derived from counts, including percentages and rates. Second, many indicators use measures of central tendency, especially the mean and the median, to paint a descriptive portrait. Third, some indicators rely on measures of dispersion, such as range and standard deviation, to convey the desired information. It is important to note that these statistics are not always used in isolation from one another. That is, an indicator may combine a measure of central tendency with a measure of dispersion in its presentation of the data, as we illustrate later in this chapter.

Common Metrics

There are a select number of statistics or metrics that indicators commonly use to convey information. The specific metrics that account for the majority of education indicators include counts, percentages, rates, percentiles, and rankings.

Before delving into descriptions of these statistics and metrics, we want to remind readers about the goals and purposes of indicators. Simply put, the goal of any indicator is to describe the status of an educational topic within a particular population. While case studies and examples are undoubtedly interesting, they rarely tell us about larger aggregate trends and patterns. It is these aggregate trends and patterns that generally represent the most meaningful representation of educational concepts and topics. Through the use of statistics and other quantitative metrics, indicators provide us with the ability to make summary statements about the collection of individuals in a population. With that in mind, we move on to discuss some statistics and metrics that are commonly used in education indicators.

Counts

Counts are simply the number of units in a population. The number of elementary and secondary school teachers in the United States is a count. Indicators that measure the number of dropouts or the number of bachelor degree recipients in the United States are based on counts. The list could go on and on. While counts are perhaps the most basic type of statistic used in education indicators, they are among the most powerful because they address the important question of "How many?"

By providing a quantitative estimate of the prevalence of a particular unit or phenomenon, counts are particularly effective in establishing the current or future importance of an issue. As a result, it will not come as a surprise that one of the most common uses of counts involves providing a sense of the scope and magnitude of perceived problems in the educational environment. For example, counts can be used to help establish an accurate perspective on crime in our schools. Figure 4.1 is based on a count, and shows the number of violent deaths (homicides and suicides) of youth ages 5–18 in school versus away from school in 2006–07. Certainly the 1,748 youth homicides are important, but the relative comparison by location tells a very dramatic story. Even with the tremendous amount of attention given to school crime, only a very small number of youth homicides occur at school. Overall, this indicator, which is based on a simple count, portrays our nation's schools as a relatively safe and nonviolent environment.

In addition to providing a perspective on the status of a current educational topic or problem, counts can be used to shape perceptions of future conditions. That is, counts are often used in the projection of future trends and for comparison with current conditions. For instance, a projection produced by the National Center for Education Statistics states that currently

Figure 4.1. Number of homicides and suicides of youth ages 5–18, by location: 2006–07

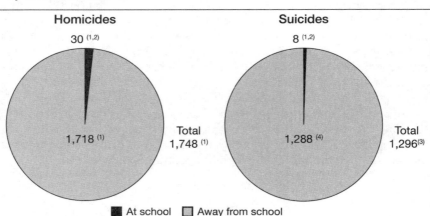

1. Youth ages 5–18 from July 1, 2006, through June 30, 2007.
2. Data from School Associated Violent Deaths Surveillance Study (SAVD) are considered preliminary.
3. Youth ages 5–18 in the 2006 calendar year.
4. This number approximates the number of suicides away from school. Use caution when interpreting this number due to timeline differences.

Note. "At school" includes on school property, on the way to or from regular sessions at school, and while attending or traveling to or from a school-sponsored event. Due to missing data for total suicides and homicides for the 2007–08 school year, this figure contains data for the 2006–07 school year. Estimates were revised and may differ from previously published data.

Source. Dinkes, R., Kemp, J., and Baum, K. (2009). Indicators of School Crime and Safety: 2009 (NCES 2010–012). Washington, DC: National Center for Education Statistics, Institute of Education Sciences, U.S. Department of Education.

there are 55.3 million students enrolled in PreK–12th grades; by 2018 there will be 59.8 million (Hussar & Bailey, 2009). This projection uses counts to illustrate that enrollment is expected to grow in future years.

In short, counts are generally used to provide an accurate depiction of the prevalence of a particular unit or phenomena of interest. Such a depiction helps to shape perceptions about the status of an educational topic or problem. Counts can be used in an absolute sense, such as the total number of teachers or bachelor's degree recipients in the United States, or they can be used in both an absolute and relative context, as was the case with the example of violent deaths of youth. Counts are clearly an invaluable and flexible method that indicators routinely use to present information.

Percentages

A *percentage* indicates the proportion of a population that exhibits a particular characteristic or behavior. Consider, for example, an indicator that states that 29% of students attending a 4-year public postsecondary institution earn a bachelor's degree in 4 years, compared with 50% of students in 4-year, private, not-for-profit institutions (Planty et al., 2009). This indicator relies on two percentages—and thus two distinct but related populations—to illustrate its point. In the first percentage, 29%, the population being represented is those students attending a 4-year public postsecondary institution. In the second percentage, 50%, the population being represented is students attending a 4-year private, not-for-profit institution. Either of these percentages could have been provided alone to describe the status of 4-year graduation with a bachelor's degree, but the developer of the indicator chose to present them together to make an explicit comparison between 4-year public postsecondary institutions and 4-year private, not-for-profit institutions. The important point to remember here is that percentages indicate the proportion of a particular population that exhibits a given characteristic or behavior, and one very important aspect of interpreting the percentage involves identifying the population being described.

Related to identifying the population being described in a percentage is judging the relative importance and impact of the particular population being described for the purpose at hand. A very large or small percentage in a particular subpopulation may have limited importance in the context of a larger population. For example, the American Indian high school dropout rate for 16–24-year-olds is very high—15% compared to the national average of 9%.[1] Clearly, this is an important problem that should be remedied. However, if the focus is on dropout rates more generally, the fact of the matter is that the total American Indian population makes up less than 1% of all public school students and subsequently about 2% of all dropouts. Extreme fluctuations in the American Indian dropout rate will have only a limited impact on the national dropout rate. This is a perfect illustration of a case where context matters significantly. If a consumer of an indicator is intent on comparing the dropout rates among different races or ethnicities within the population, then the dropout rate among American Indians is a very important component of this goal. However, if the goal of the consumer is to gauge how the dropout rates of various groups contribute to the national dropout rate, then knowledge of the dropout rate among American Indian students is only somewhat useful.

Related to percentages is the concept of percentage change. This important concept provides a quantitative gauge as to how something has

Table 4.1. New York State elementary and secondary enrollment:
1970–71 through 2007–08

Sector/ grade group	1970–71	1980–81	1990–91	2000–01	2007–08	Percentage change 1970–2008	Percentage change 2000–2008
Total	**4,277,098**	**3,418,257**	**3,024,365**	**3,324,100**	**3,163,171**	**-26.0**	**-4.8**
K–6	2,402,858	1,716,317	1,703,037	1,855,456	1,642,991	-31.6	-11.5
7–12	1,874,240	1,701,940	1,321,328	1,468,644	1,520,180	-18.9	3.5
Public	**3,489,245**	**2,838,393**	**2,547,258**	**2,828,362**	**2,714,385**	**-22.2**	**-4.0**
K–6	1,939,976	1,384,286	1,419,001	1,562,045	1,401,912	-27.7	-10.3
7–12	1,549,269	1,454,107	1,128,257	1,266,317	1,312,473	-15.3	3.6

Source. Data taken from New York State Education Department (NYSED). (2010). *Education Statistics for New York State.* New York, NY: Author. Retrieved March 9, 2010, from http://www.emsc.nysed.gov/irts/statistics/public/table1.html

changed over time. Specifically, *percentage change* is the percentage increase or decrease from an initial base year to another point in time. Calculating the percentage change involves starting with two values at two points in time, subtracting the older value from the newer value, and then dividing by the older value. This number is then multiplied by 100 to get the percentage change. For example, Table 4.1 details the percentage change in enrollment for New York State between 1971 and 2008. To provide a concrete example of calculating percentage change, we examine the statistic indicating that enrollment declined by 26.0% from 1970 to 2008. To calculate this statistic, subtract the enrollment in 2007–08 from enrollment in 1970–71 (3,163,171 − 4,277,098 = -1,113,927). Then, divide the result by enrollment in 1970–71 and multiply by 100 to get the percentage change (-1,113,927 / 4,277,098 = -0.260 x 100 = -26.0).

Percentage change can provide an effective description of change over time, but there are some factors that can cause startling results when calculating percentage changes. Specifically, small population sizes or starting values can produce dramatic percentage change estimates. As a result, it is important to have an awareness and understanding of the basis for the percentage change calculations. To illustrate some of the pitfalls, we provide a contextual example. Table 4.2 shows the number of postsecondary degrees conferred by institution type and calculates the percentage change from 1996–97 to 2006–07. It immediately jumps out that for-profit institutions had a 900% increase in the number of master's degrees conferred between 1997 and 2007, compared to only 25% for public institutions.

Table 4.2. Number and percentage change of degrees conferred by degree-granting institutions, by control of institution and type of degree: 1996–97 to 2006–07

Type of degree and academic year	Total	Public	Private Total	Private Not-for-Profit	For-Profit
Associate's					
1996–97	571,226	465,494	105,732	49,168	56,564
2006–07	728,114	566,535	161,579	43,829	117,750
Percent change	27	22	53	-11	108
Bachelor's					
1996–97	1,172,879	776,677	396,202	384,086	12,116
2006–07	1,524,092	975,513	548,579	477,805	70,774
Percent change	30	26	38	24	484
Master's					
1996–97	419,401	233,237	186,164	181,104	5,060
2006–07	604,607	291,971	312,636	261,700	50,936
Percent change	44	25	68	45	907
First-professional					
1996–97	78,730	31,243	47,487	47,029	458
2006–07	90,064	36,855	53,209	52,746	463
Percent change	14	18	12	12	1
Doctoral					
1996–97	45,876	29,838	16,038	15,694	344
2006–07	60,616	36,230	24,386	22,483	1,903
Percent change	32	21	52	43	453

Sources. U.S. Department of Education, National Center for Education Statistics, 1996–97 and 2006–07 IPEDS, "Completions Survey" (IPEDS-C:97) and Fall 2007.

What is going on with for-profit institutions and master's degrees? Closer inspection reveals that for-profit institutions accounted for only about 1% of the 419,401 master's degrees awarded in 1997, which translates to about 5,000 degrees. In comparison, public institutions conferred about 56% of the 419,401 master's degrees awarded in 1997, or over 230,000 degrees.

While for-profit institutions are certainly growing at a faster rate, they are also starting with a much smaller base, which can inflate the percentage change. It is important to note that the 906% increase in master's degrees awarded by for-profit institutions translates to about 45,000 additional degrees. In contrast, the 25% increase in master's degrees conferred by public institutions translates to an additional 58,700 degrees. Consumers of indicators must be aware of situations such as these when interpreting percentage change statistics.

Rates

Rates are a third metric that indicators commonly use to convey information. A *rate* is calculated as the ratio of two numbers, and can be interpreted as the number of events that occur in a specified common unit. The common unit could be a given amount of time (events per year), a set number of people (events per 1,000 students), or any other unit that the developer of the indicator specifies. Rates provide a way of standardizing data and thus presenting a more meaningful picture or comparison.

Perhaps the most common standardization involves accounting for differences in population size between groups. Take, for example, an indicator that describes school crime victimization by racial/ethnic group, which we display below in Table 4.3. If a consumer of this indicator were to look at the simple count of crimes (presented in the first four columns of the table), he would conclude that Whites experience much more crime than either Black or Hispanic students. For instance, White students suffered 955,800 crimes at school, compared to 266,300 for Blacks and 267,400 for Hispanics. So, it is true that, in the aggregate, Whites experience much more crime than Blacks or Hispanics. But is this the best comparison? There are many more White students in the country than Black or Hispanic students. What would happen if we examine the rate of crime experienced by each racial/ethnic group? The right bank of the table presents the rate of crime per 1,000 students. It is clear that when we express the number of crimes experienced by each racial/ethnic group as a rate, as opposed to a count, a completely different picture emerges. Specifically, we observe higher total, violent, and serious violent victimization rates for Blacks compared with their White peers. Conclusions based on crimes experienced per 1,000 students differ greatly from conclusions based on simple counts of crimes experienced.

Percentiles

Percentiles are a fourth metric that indicators commonly use to convey information. Percentile data measure the status of individuals in a popula-

Table 4.3. Number of student-reported nonfatal crimes against students ages 12–18 and rate of crimes per 1,000 students at school, by type of crime and race or ethnicity of student: 2006

Race/ ethnicity	Number of crimes				Rate of crimes per 1,000 students			
	Total	Theft	Violent	Serious violent	Total	Theft	Violent	Serious violent
White	955,800	530,300	425,500	84,800	60	33	27	5
Black	266,300	134,100	132,200	33,500	65	33	32	8
Hispanic	267,400	140,300	127,100	38,000	56	29	26	8

Source. U.S. Department of Justice, Bureau of Justice Statistics, *National Crime Victimization Survey (NCVS)*, 2006.

tion at different points of the outcome distribution. A *percentile* is defined as the percentage of the population below a specified point on a given distribution. Percentiles are encountered most frequently in indicators that report on student achievement. As a result, we will use an example from that context to demonstrate the use of percentile data. Figure 4.2 presents the scale score on the National Assessment of Educational Progress mathematics assessment for 17-year-olds at the 10th, 25th, 50th, 75th, and 90th percentiles of the achievement distribution from 1978 through 2008. To provide a bit of context, if a student scores at the 10th percentile in 2008, it means that only 10% of the population have a score below their score of 267. Similarly, if a student scores at the 90th percentile of the distribution in 2008, it means that that score of 343 is better than the scores of 90% of the population.

It is important to remember that percentiles do not convey an inherent substantive or absolute meaning, but simply rank individuals relative to all others in a given population. Imagine, for example, that an indicator presents percentile data on standardized test scale scores for the population of students in a gifted and talented program. In this hypothetical indicator, students at the 90th percentile would score better than students at the 10th percentile, but it is likely that all students in this sample would score very well if they were compared to the larger population of all students and not just those in gifted and talented programs. Remember, percentile data only compare students within a given population. Such data say nothing about the absolute performance levels of individuals.

Finally, while percentile data are most commonly seen in the context of standardized test performance, they are certainly not limited to this context. Almost any topic has an outcome distribution that is amenable to being described by percentile data. For example, an indicator could present infor-

Figure 4.2. NAEP mathematics percentile scale scores for 17-year-old students: 1978–2008

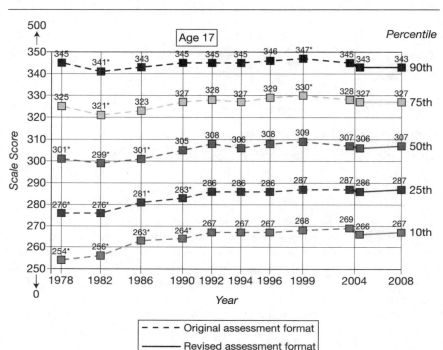

* Significantly different (p <. 05) from 2008.

Source. U.S. Department of Education, Institute of Education Sciences, National Center for Education Statistics, National Assessment of Educational Progress (NAEP), various years, 1978–2008 Long-Term Trend Mathematics Assessments.

mation on per-pupil expenditures at various, chosen percentiles. Similarly, an indicator could provide data on teacher salaries at selected percentiles. In sum, any topic with a distribution of outcomes can be described using percentile data.

Rankings

A number of indicators present their data in the form of *rankings,* which are simply an ordering of units. Rankings are ubiquitous in all areas of our lives, and education is no exception. In education, rankings are used in school, state, and international comparisons. As an example of school-level rankings, colleges and universities routinely advertise the ranking assigned to them by the *U.S. News and World Report* annual rankings. At the state level, the U.S. Department of Education releases the average score on the National Assessment of Educational Progress for each state. While the Department of Education does not explicitly rank states, the presentation of state scores allows for informal rankings. Similarly, the Center for Education Reform (2009) ranks states in terms of the strength of their laws addressing charter schools. In the international context, a number of assessments—such as the Program for International Student Assessment and Trends in International Mathematics and Science Study—rank student performance in the United States relative to student performance in other countries. The allure of rankings is easy to understand; everyone wants to know who is performing best and who is not doing so well. Rankings provide quick, concise comparisons of units, and these features are quite appealing.

Despite their appeal, rankings also possess some disadvantages. The problems center on the quality of the measures used to generate the ranking, year-to-year variation, the choice of comparison groups, and qualitative differences between rankings. To illustrate some of the potential drawbacks of rankings, consider U.S. student performance on the two international mathematics assessments mentioned above, the Program for International Student Assessment (PISA) and the Trends in International Mathematics and Science Study (TIMSS). Table 4.4 details the U.S. score relative to a set of participating countries. Setting aside differences in the student testing population and the purpose of each test, a naive assessment would conclude that the U.S. ranked 9th out of 48 countries on the TIMSS and 25th out of 30 countries on the PISA assessment. How can these two assessments of the same subject reach such drastically different conclusions? There are a couple of factors that can contribute to the varying conclusions. First, it is important to note that the estimated scale scores for each country are based on a sample of students, and as a result they have a margin of error (see the section on sampling error later in this chapter). Taking that margin of error into account for TIMSS, we can only be sure that 5 jurisdictions outperformed the United States—Chinese Taipei, Korea, Singapore, Hong Kong, and Japan (signified by the up arrows in the chart). Similarly, the U.S. score is not statistically different from the scores of 5 additional countries (Hungary, England, Russia, Lithuania, and the Czech Republic). Finally, we can be sure that student performance in the United States was better than student performance in 37 countries (those signified by the down arrows). A comparable situation occurs on PISA. Once we take the margin of error associated with estimating student performance into account, we can only be sure that 23 countries outperformed the United States, two countries had scores that were not statistically different, and the United States outper-

Table 4.4. Average PISA scores of 15-year-old students on mathematics literacy scale and average TIMSS scores of eighth-grade students in mathematics

TIMSS			PISA		
Jurisdiction	Average score		Jurisdiction	Average score	
All jurisdictions	**500**	↓	**All OECD jurisdictions**	**498**	↑
			OECD		
1 Chinese Taipei	598	↑	1 Finland	548	↑
2 Korea, Republic of	597	↑	2 Korea, Republic of	547	↑
3 Singapore	593	↑	3 Netherlands	531	↑
4 Hong Kong SAR	572	↑	4 Switzerland	530	↑
5 Japan	570	↑	5 Canada	527	↑
6 Hungary	517		6 Japan	523	↑
7 England	513		7 New Zealand	522	↑
8 Russian Federation	512		8 Belgium	520	↑
9 **United States**	**508**		9 Australia	520	↑
10 Lithuania	506		10 Denmark	513	↑
11 Czech Republic	504		11 Czech Republic	510	↑
12 Slovenia	501	↓	12 Iceland	506	↑
13 Armenia	499	↓	13 Austria	505	↑
14 Australia	496	↓	14 Germany	504	↑
15 Sweden	491	↓	15 Sweden	502	↑
16 Malta	488	↓	16 Ireland	501	↑
17 Scotland	487	↓	17 France	496	↑
18 Serbia	486	↓	18 United Kingdom	495	↑
19 Italy	480	↓	19 Poland	495	↑
20 Malaysia	474	↓	20 Slovak Republic	492	↑
21 Norway	469	↓	21 Hungary	491	↑
22 Cyprus	465	↓	22 Luxembourg	490	↑
23 Bulgaria	464	↓	23 Norway	490	↑
24 Israel	463	↓	24 Spain	480	↓
25 Ukraine	462	↓	25 **United States**	**474**	↓
26 Romania	461	↓	26 Portugal	466	↓
27 Bosnia and Herzegovina	456	↓	27 Italy	462	↓
28 Lebanon	449	↓	28 Greece	459	↓
29 Thailand	441	↓	29 Turkey	424	↓
30 Turkey	432	↓	30 Mexico	406	↓
31 Jordan	427	↓			
32 Tunisia	420	↓			
33 Georgia	410	↓			
34 Iran, Islamic Republic of	403	↓			
35 Bahrain	398	↓			
36 Indonesia	397	↓			
37 Syrian Arab Republic	395	↓			
38 Egypt	391	↓			
39 Algeria	387	↓			
40 Colombia	380	↓			
41 Oman	372	↓			
42 Palestinian National Authority	367	↓			
43 Botswana	364	↓			
44 Kuwait	354	↓			
45 El Salvador	340	↓			
46 Saudi Arabia	329	↓			
47 Ghana	309	↓			
48 Qatar	307	↓			

↑ Score is higher than U.S. score. ↓ Score is lower than U.S. score.

Source. Gonzales, P., Williams, T., Jocelyn, L., Roey, S., Kastberg, D., and Brenwald, S. (2008). Highlights from TIMSS 2007: Mathematics and Science Achievement of U.S. Fourth- and Eighth-Grade Students in an International Context (NCES 2009–001), tables 3 and 9. National Center for Education Statistics, Institute of Education Sciences, U.S. Department of Education. Washington, DC.; and Organization for Economic Cooperation and Development (OECD). (2007). *PISA 2006: Science Competencies for Tomorrow's World, Volume 2: Data,* table 6.2c. Paris: Author.

formed 4 countries. The point here is to note that the margin of error associated with estimating scores (or any other outcome) can have an impact on the conclusions that are drawn regarding rankings (Stoneberg, 2005).

Second, it is important to realize that while each mathematics assessment purports to rank the United States in an international context, each assessment program uses a very different set of countries for comparison. The lower ranking of the United States on PISA is partially attributable to the fact that the set of comparison countries is primarily composed of developed nations with well-established education systems and labor markets. The group of countries participating in TIMSS includes several countries with less developed education systems and labor markets. Using different numbers and types of comparison groups will lead to different rankings regardless of the actual student performance.

Finally, we want to briefly address the topic of interpreting the scale and assessing the qualitative difference between groups. On TIMSS, the United States scored 90 points lower than the top-performing Chinese Taipei, 8 points higher than the international average and 201 points higher than Qatar. What does this all mean? How does one translate the ranking and scores into something more substantive? How much more do the Chinese Taipei students know than U.S. students? Rankings are not generally well suited to answer such a question. Most ranking systems provide little more than a relative guide to one's position in a population and when presented alone often struggle to provide much substantive meaning.

Measures of Central Tendency

The metrics described above—counts, percentages, rates, percentiles, and rankings—are common approaches to summarizing and presenting complex data in education. As our examples demonstrated, they serve as the basis for a wide variety of education indicators that provide significant value to policy makers and researchers. While these metrics are commonly encountered, they are hardly the only metrics that serve as the basis for education indicators. Indeed, indicators often use additional metrics to describe the status of a topic or problem in the educational environment. Measures of central tendency—mean, median, and mode—represent the average outcome for a population.

Mean

When people talk about the "average"—whether it is an average score on a test, the average age of college students, or some other topic of interest—they are generally referring to the mean. The *mean* for a population is cal-

Table 4.5. Percentage distribution of undergraduates by age group and institution sector: 2007–08

			Percent		
Type of Institution	Mean Age	Median Age	15–23	24–29	30+
All colleges	26	22	60	17	23
Community colleges	28	23	50	19	31
Public 4-year colleges	23	21	74	14	12
Private not-for-profit 4-year colleges	24	20	70	12	18

Source. U.S. Department of Education, National Center for Education Statistics, *2007–08 National Postsecondary Student Aid Study* (NPSAS:08).

culated by adding all values and dividing the sum by the total number of data points. As an example of an indicator that relies on the mean, consider Table 4.5. It is often stated that community colleges serve a very different population of students than 4-year institutions. Is this true? Looking at the table, we find some support for this proposition. The mean age of students attending community colleges is 28, which is older than the mean age of their peers at 4-year public and private not-for-profit institutions, who have a mean age of 23 and 24, respectively. Here, the mean age provides some support for the conjecture that community colleges serve a different population than 4-year institutions.

Like any metric, the mean has a unique set of advantages and disadvantages. There are three main advantages of the mean: (1) It is a single number that is very familiar and easily interpretable; (2) it can be calculated for almost any topic or outcome of interest; and (3) it uses all observations to produce a reliable estimate of the population average. There are two primary disadvantages with the mean: (1) As a single number it may not do a good job representing the distribution of values in the population and (2) it can be affected by extreme values or outliers. To illustrate the potential drawbacks of using the mean, we again consider the indicator describing the average age of college attendees by type of institution (see Table 4.5). The indicator shows that the mean age of community college attendees is 28. However, when looking at the percentage distribution in the three columns to the right, it becomes evident that community colleges tend to have a lot of younger and older students; community colleges appear to have relatively few attendees between 24 and 29 years of age. By simply looking at the mean age, consumers of the indicator may conclude that most students are about 28 years old. A more in-depth analysis reveals that the mean age may indeed be 28, but relatively few students attending community college are in that age range; students tend to be younger or older and the combination of these groups produces a mean age of 28.

Median

The median is another common measure of central tendency. The *median* is simply the middle value in a group of data. At the median value, exactly half of the observations exhibit lower values and half exhibit higher values. A primary virtue of the median is that, unlike the mean, it is not affected by extreme cases or outliers. As a result, the median is often used in cases where outliers could affect the conclusions that may be drawn from an indicator.

To illustrate a comparison between the mean and the median, we use a hypothetical example of the serious violent incident count for a set of 9 hypothetical schools in District Y (see Table 4.6). In Group A, we see very little variation between schools; the mean, median, and mode are all in the same ballpark. In this case, using any or all of these measures of central tendency would be acceptable. However, now consider Group B. In this group School 9 has a value of 25, instead of a value of 3. This causes the mean to jump from 2 to 4. Such a jump is problematic because none of the other 8 schools have a value greater than 3. In this case, the mean is not a useful measure for the "average" school. The median and mode—with values of 2 and 3, respectively—tend to perform better as measures of central tendency in this type of scenario.

One common use of the median in indicators is with topics related to salaries. In many cases, a small group of people earn a lot more money than most people, and these outliers can distort the central tendency in a mean (think of Bill Gates and Warren Buffet in relation to your own salary). While outliers may affect the mean when looking at a general distribution of salaries, some salary comparisons are not overly prone to outliers. Teacher pay is often determined by a very strict salary schedule that is wholly based on years of service and education attainment. For example, Maryland's Montgomery County public school teacher salary schedule, which is presented in Table 4.7, demonstrates a rather narrow, finite band of salaries that are not prone to extreme values. The entire schedule is contained between a low of $46,410 and a high of $103,634. In such cases, the mean and median values are likely to be very close. It becomes important to understand the full range and distribution of the estimate before choosing your measure. A simple diagnostic is to compare one measure of central tendency to another. If the measures perform

Table 4.6. Hypothetical District Y with 9
schools: Number of serious violent incidents,
by measures of central tendency and dispersion

	Incidents A	Incidents B
School 1	0	0
School 2	0	0
School 3	1	1
School 4	1	1
School 5	2	2
School 6	3	3
School 7	3	3
School 8	3	3
School 9	3	25
Mean	2	4
Median	2	2
Mode	3	3
Range	3	25
Variance	2	62
Standard deviation	1	7

similarly, it is probably OK to use either one, and the mean may be preferable because of its familiarity. If the measures perform differently, however, it is the responsibility of the developer of the indicator to determine which measure best represents the central tendency of the data.

Mode

A third common measure of central tendency, the *mode* is simply the value that is observed most frequently in a set of data. Compared to the mean and the median, the mode is used relatively infrequently in education indicators. Its lack of use is largely attributable to the nature of education data. Data in the field of education are often continuous in nature (think of test scores or teacher salaries); they often vary widely and lack repeat values. As an example, Table 4.8 presents state-level high school graduation rates, which can range from 0–100 %. This group of data would have three

Table 4.7. Teacher salary schedule, Montgomery County, Maryland: 2010

	BA	MA/MEQ	MA+30	MA+60
	Teacher/Other Positions Effective July 1, 2009 (Max entrance step)			
1	$46,410	$51,128	$52,630	$53,990
2	$47,125	$51,986	$54,200	$55,562
3	$48,538	$53,987	$56,286	$57,701
4	$49,995	$56,066	$58,454	$59,922
5	$51,494	$58,225	$60,704	$62,229
6	$53,478	$60,466	$63,041	$64,625
7	$55,537	$62,794	$65,469	$67,114
8	$57,674	$65,212	$67,990	$69,697
9	$59,895	$67,723	$70,607	$72,381
10	$62,201	$70,330	$73,325	$75,167
11		$73,038	$76,148	$78,061
12		$75,850	$79,079	$81,066
13		$78,770	$82,124	$84,187
14		$81,802	$85,285	$87,428
15		$84,256	$87,844	$90,051
16		$86,785	$90,480	$92,753
17		$89,388	$93,194	$95,535
18		$92,069	$95,990	$98,402
19–24		$94,832	$98,870	$101,354
25		$96,966	$101,095	$103,634

Source. Data taken from Montgomery County Public Schools (MCPS). (2009). Teacher salary schedule. Rockville, MD: Author. Retrieved March 9, 2010, from http://www.montgomeryschoolsmd.org/departments/ersc/docs/Salary_Schedules_FY10_MCEA.pdf

modes—86.5%, 76.6%, and 71.9%—since two states have each of those values. As a measure of central tendency, the mode is not very useful in this case. The fact that there are three modes and each mode is shared by only two states makes it difficult to assess the "typical" graduation rate using this metric.

The mode is most useful in situations where there are a limited number of mutually exclusive response categories. For example, looking at Table 4.9, we see that the category "specific learning disabilities" is the modal category. That is, it is the most often cited disability among 3–21-year-olds served by the Individuals with Disabilities Education Act. In this case, the mode provides useful information to the consumer of the indicator.

Table 4.8. Averaged freshman graduation rates, by state: 2006–07

State	AFGR	State	AFGR	State	AFGR
Vermont	88.6	Kansas	78.9	Tennessee	72.6
Wisconsin	88.5	Ohio	78.7	Delaware	71.9
Iowa	86.5	Maine	78.5	Texas	71.9
Minnesota	86.5	Rhode Island	78.4	California	70.7
Nebraska	86.3	West Virginia	78.2	Arizona	69.6
New Jersey	84.4	Oklahoma	77.8	Alaska	69.1
North Dakota	83.1	Michigan	77.0	New York	68.8
Pennsylvania	83.0	Colorado	76.6	North Carolina	68.6
South Dakota	82.5	Utah	76.6	Alabama	67.1
Missouri	81.9	Kentucky	76.4	Florida	65.0
Connecticut	81.8	Wyoming	75.8	Georgia	64.1
New Hampshire	81.7	Virginia	75.5	Mississippi	63.6
Montana	81.5	Hawaii	75.4	Louisiana	61.3
Massachusetts	80.8	Washington	74.8	New Mexico	59.1
Idaho	80.4	Arkansas	74.4	South Carolina	58.9
Maryland	80.0	Indiana	73.9	D.C.	54.9
Illinois	79.5	Oregon	73.8	Nevada	52.0

Source. Stillwell, R. (2009). *Public School Graduates and Dropouts from the Common Core of Data: School Year 2006–07* (NCES 2010-313). National Center for Education Statistics, Institute of Education Sciences, U.S. Department of Education. Washington, DC.

Measures of Dispersion

From the previous section on measures of control tendency, we know that an "average" value only provides information about the outcome for the individual or unit in the middle of the outcome distribution. Measures of dispersion assess the spread of the outcome. That is, they tell us whether the outcomes are spread over a broad range or if they are concentrated in a relatively narrow band. As the example dealing with the age of college attendees illustrated (see Table 4.5), there are many values both above and below the middle of the distribution. Knowing how the values are spread above and below the middle of the distribution is often just as informative as knowing the mean or median value. Indeed, in the example describing the age of

Table 4.9. Number of 3- to 21-year-olds served under Individuals with Disabilities Education Act (IDEA), by type of disability: 2007–08

All disabilities	6,605,724
Type of disability	
Specific learning disabilities	2,573,059
Speech or language impairments	1,456,347
Mental retardation	499,857
Emotional disturbance	441,847
Hearing impairments	78,987
Orthopedic impairments	67,436
Other health impairments	641,061
Visual impairments	29,041
Deaf-blindness	1,502
Autism	295,940
Traumatic brain injury	24,679
Developmental delay	357,825
Multiple disabilities	138,143

Each category is mutually exclusive and represents the number of students served.

Source. U.S. Department of Education, Office of Special Education Programs, Annual Report to Congress on the Implementation of the Individuals with Disabilities Education Act, Individuals with Disabilities Education Act (IDEA) database, retrieved April 14, 2009, from www.ideadata.org/PartBdata.asp.

college attendees, we saw that many students attending community college were either well above or well below the average age of attendees, which was 28. Fortunately, there are several measures of dispersion that capture the spread or shape of outcome values around the central tendency. These measures of dispersion can tell us whether the outcome values are tightly concentrated or widely dispersed. We discuss four of them here: the range, the variance, the standard deviation, and the coefficient of variation.

Range

The most common, and simplest, measure of dispersion is the range. The *range* is the difference between the lowest and highest values, and is often included in an indicator. As an example of the range, consider again Table 4.8, which presented state-level high school graduation rates in 2006–07. In this table, the state with the lowest value is Nevada, where only 52% of students graduate. The state with the highest graduation rate is Vermont, where 89% of students graduate. In this example, state-level graduation rates range from a low of 52% to a high of 89%, so the range is 37 percentage points.

Variance

A second measure of dispersion—variance—is only occasionally used in education indicators because it is more complex and not directly interpretable. Still, consumers of education indicators might encounter the variance on occasion, so we provide a very brief definition here: *Variance* is the average squared difference of each observation from the mean. A more common metric used to describe the variability is the standard deviation.

Standard Deviation

A very common measure of dispersion is the standard deviation. Closely related to the variance, the *standard deviation* is, in fact, the square root of the variance. Unlike the variance, however, the standard deviation is more substantively meaningful. In most situations, 95% of observations have values that are between two standard deviations below the mean and two standard deviations above the mean. To illustrate the concept of the standard deviation, consider a hypothetical standardized test where the mean student score is 70 and the standard deviation has been calculated to be 10. Because we know the mean and the standard deviation, we know that 95% of test scores will fall between the values of 50 and 90. If the standard deviation were smaller, say 5 instead of 10, then 95% of test scores would fall between 60 and 80, rather than 50 and 90. A small standard deviation means that the values are more tightly concentrated around the mean, while a large standard deviation means that the values are more broadly dispersed. We briefly return to the concept of the standard deviation in the section on statistical testing later in this chapter.

Coefficient of Variation

A final measure of dispersion that is occasionally encountered in education indicators is the coefficient of variation (CV). The *coefficient of variation* is the ratio of the standard deviation to the mean. Highly varied populations will have a large CV, and when an indicator exhibits a relatively high CV, consumers should be cautious about the reliability and precision of the indicator. Typically, a CV of 50% or more is considered high, but there is no accepted level adopted by the research community. The CV is often used to bring attention to estimates that have high levels of variability and further investigations should determine whether this is a reflection of reality or a product of sampling.

Summary of Statistical Measures

Indicators most often rely on counts, percentages, percentiles, rates, or rankings to present data on the topic they intend to portray. In addition, indicators also commonly make use of measures of central tendency and dispersion. Measures of central tendency describe the typical or average response whereas measures of dispersion, which are used less in indicator reports but are just as critical, describe the variation and spread within a population. There are a few guidelines when using these measures: means are often affected by extreme outliers and modes are best for categorical data. Beyond that, one must examine the data and distributions carefully and use the most appropriate measure for the purpose at hand. In many cases it is best to use multiple measures, and evaluation is best left to the analyst as to the appropriateness and value of a particular measure.

STATISTICAL TESTING AND STATISTICAL SIGNIFICANCE

In Chapter 3 we discussed the differences associated with using data collected from a sample (sample data) versus from the entire population (universe data). We noted that an important disadvantage of sampling is sampling error, which is the error or imprecision that stems from taking a sample of the population rather than a complete enumeration of the whole population. The size of this sampling error will depend on the variation in the population and the sampling strategy employed.

What does the existence of sampling error mean for indicators? At the most basic level, it means that for every estimate based on data from a sample, there is some margin of error associated with it. In indicators based on universe data, the number presented is considered to be the true value in the population. However, in indicators based on sample data the estimate presented is not considered to be the true value in the population, but instead the "best guess" of the true value in the population; the true value in the population is thought to fall in a range around the estimate, but the true value cannot be known with certainty. To provide a contextual example, consider again the example of the indicator that described the average age of college attendees (refer to Table 4.5). This indicator estimated the average age of community college attendees to be 28. However, this estimate was based on data collected from a sample of the population. As a result, the true average age of community college attendees is actually unknown, but the best guess is 28. We can be fairly certain that the true average age of community college attendees in the population is within a specified range around 28. That specified range is referred to as the *confidence interval,* and we discuss it in a bit more detail later point in this section. In the end, samples force us to give up some level of precision and reliability in exchange for savings in the time, costs, and other sources of error associated with surveying the entire population.

Constructing population estimates from data based on a sample can also complicate efforts to make comparisons between groups. For example, we might be interested in knowing whether the average age of community college attendees is different for students who are White versus students who are Black. Similarly, we might want to know whether the average age of community college students today is higher than it was in 1970. With universe data, making such comparisons is relatively easy. It simply involves comparing the estimates for each group and observing whether there is a difference. If there is, it can be concluded that the two groups really do differ in the population. Such comparisons become a bit more complicated, however, when the estimates are constructed from sample data. When estimates are constructed from sample data we need to account for sampling error when determining whether the groups really differ from each other. In many cases, we cannot be sure that two estimates that on their face are different from each other are truly different in the population. Our uncertainty regarding the difference in estimates stems from the fact that the estimates are only our best guesses of the true value in the population. We are fairly certain that the true population value for each group lies in a range around their respective estimates. However, if the ranges for the two (or more) groups we are comparing overlap, this means we cannot be certain that the values for the two groups actually differ in the population.

Statistical Testing

When estimates are constructed from samples, how can we be relatively sure that the values for two groups in the population are actually different? Whenever we are interested in any group comparisons and the estimates for the groups are based on samples, we employ statistical testing to determine whether differences exist. *Statistical testing* can be quite complicated, but in its most basic form it is an attempt to decide whether the observed difference between two groups is likely to be "real" or simply due to sampling error. Remember, estimates produced by universe surveys do not have sampling error, so statistical testing is unnecessary.

Using the point estimate and the standard error, a very common way to determine whether the differences between the means or percentages between two groups are statistically significant is to use a *t*-test. There are four possible outcomes when statistically testing an observed difference between the estimates of two groups A and B:

- Group A is greater than group B
- Group B is greater than group A
- No difference detected between groups A and B
- The samples do not permit a reliable statistical test

Whether an observed difference is determined to be statistically significant depends on the *p*-value that is returned from a statistical test, such as a *t*-test. The *p*-value is our degree of certainty that the observed differences between two population estimates are true differences and cannot be attributed to sampling error. The *p*-value ranges from 0 to 1 and lower *p*-values indicate greater certainty that the observed difference cannot be attributed to sampling error.

The threshold for statistical significance is determined by the researcher. The general convention in most government reports and research articles is to test for statistical significance at the $p < .05$ level, but .01 and .001 are also common. A finding reported at the .01 level is interpreted as more confident than one at the .05 level. At the .05 level, we are saying that 5 out of 100 repeated samples would produce this finding by chance. So at the .01 level, we are choosing a more rigorous standard and reducing the uncertainty to 1 out of 100 trials. However, computers and software programs are now able to generate the exact p-values for every estimate, and that is the most transparent form of documentation to use.

Standard Error and Confidence Intervals

One measure used in statistical testing is the "standard error," which is a quantitative estimate of the error that may occur because of sampling. Because the estimate is constructed from data collected from a sample of the population, we do not know the true value in the population. However, the standard error allows us to construct a range in which we are relatively sure the true value in the population falls, a range known as the *confidence interval*. Often 90% or 95% confidence intervals are created around point estimates. Although we will not go into detail about the construction of confidence intervals, we emphasize that the confidence interval represents a range of values within which the true population value falls with a given

Table 4.10. Number of all school-age children who were homeschooled:
1999, 2003, and 2007

	1999	2003	2007
Count	850,000	1,096,000	1,508,000
Standard error	71,100	92,300	117,900
95% confidence interval	709,000–992,000	915,000–1,277,000	1,277,000–1,739,000

Source. U.S. Department of Education, National Center for Education Statistics, Parent Survey of the
1999 National Household Education Surveys Program (NHES), Parent and Family Involvement in
Education Survey of the 2003 and 2007 NHES. Available at http://nces.ed.gov/pubs2009/2009030.pdf

level of confidence. The smaller the standard error, the more confident we
can be that the estimate of the population value is close to the true population value. When standard errors are large, we cannot be very confident that
the estimate, which is best guess of the value in the population, is close to
the true population value.

To illustrate the concept of statistical testing, we use an example from
the National Household Education Survey (NHES) conducted by the NCES.
The NHES is a sample survey of households across the nation where residents are asked questions on a variety of topics related to education, including their educational status and attainment. One set of questions asks
whether any children in the household are homeschooled. These responses
are used to create national estimates for the number and percentage of children who are homeschooled in the United States. In Table 4.10 shows that
the estimate of the number of children who are homeschooled increased
from 850,000 to 1.5 million between 1999 and 2007.

The table also gives the standard error and confidence intervals for each
year. For 1999 the 95% confidence interval ranges from 709,000 to 992,000.
We can interpret this to mean, that if we repeated the NHES sample multiple times in an identical manner the confidence interval would include the
true population value 95% of the time. In other words, we can be 95%
confident that the number of students homeschooled in 1999 is somewhere
between 709,000 and 992,000 students. Similarly, the confidence interval
for the number of students homeschooled in 2007 ranges from 1.2 million
students to 1.7 million students. This range is useful, but a confidence interval of 500,000 students seems rather large, and this level of precision may
not be very satisfying for some purposes. As we have repeatedly stressed
throughout this book, it is the responsibility of the consumer of the indicator to assess whether estimates based on sample data have enough precision
for the purpose at hand.

Standard Error: Sample Size and Variance

Two general factors determine the size of the sampling error: sample size[2] and the amount of variance in the outcome within the population. So what does this mean for indicators? First, all else being equal, larger sample sizes are associated with smaller standard errors. This seems intuitive because as the sample approaches the actual population size, it is more likely that the sample reflects the actual population value. In the example above, the homeschooling estimates have rather large standard errors. This is, in part, due to the fact that these estimates are based on only 290 sample members out of the 10,681 respondents interviewed. Consumers must always use caution when estimates are based on very small sample sizes. Larger standard errors, of course, result in less reliability in the estimate, and we are thus less likely to detect a difference between two groups.

Of course, there is nothing the analyst or reader can do about large standard errors that result from small sample sizes. The sample was drawn and the data collected. The other factor affecting standard errors is the inherent variability in the outcome in the population. If everyone behaves or responds identically, then there is less variability in the estimate than there would be if respondents behaved or responded in a varying manner. Again, it is intuitive that certainty in the true population value will be reduced if respondents behave differently relative to a situation where respondents behave similarly.

OTHER CONSIDERATIONS FOR EVALUATING INDICATOR QUALITY

Substantive Significance

Even when you are certain that two groups in the population are statistically different or, in the case of universe data, when each difference is considered real, it is also critical to explore *substantive significance*. That is, it is important to examine whether the differences between the groups are meaningful and important. For example, consider the indicator presented in Figure 4.3 that describes the average mathematics scores for male and female fourth graders. While it is not readily apparent from the figure, the average score for male students (241) is statistically different from the average score of female students (239) with a gap of 2 points in 2009. After determining that the scores for the two groups are statistically different, it is important to determine whether the difference is substantively meaningful.

Figure 4.3. Average eighth-grade mathematics scale scores, by gender and race/ethnicity: 1990–2009

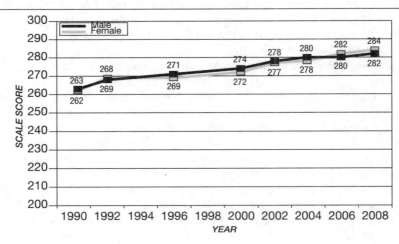

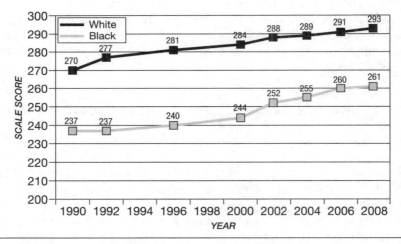

Note. National Assessment of Educational Progress (NAEP) mathematics scores range from 0 to 500.

Source. U.S. Department of Education, National Center for Education Statistics, National Assessment of Educational Progress (NAEP), selected years, 1990–2009 Mathematics Assessments, NAEP Data Explorer.

In the case of the average score by gender, most people would probably conclude that the gender difference is not very important. While statistically significant, a 2-point gap on the NAEP 500-point scale is not very large. In fact, both scores, 239 and 241, map onto the middle of the NAEP basic proficiency level. Another way to determine whether a group difference is substantively meaningful is to compare it to other group differences. In this example, we can compare gender differences to race/ethnicity differences. When we examine the average mathematics scores by student race/ethnicity, we find gaps of 20 to 30 points on the same 500-point NAEP scale. In 2009 the average scale score of 222 for Black students appears at the lower end of the NAEP basic level, while the average White score of 248 appears just under the NAEP proficient level cut point of 249. Clearly, when compared to race/ethnicity differences, the gender differences do not appear large at all. This example illustrates a case where two sets of group differences can both be statistically significant, but their substantive importance differs.

As has been the case with many other aspects of indicators, there is no hard-and-fast method for assessing whether a difference between two groups in the population is substantively significant. Assessments of substantive significance are influenced by context and the purposes of the analyst or consumer of the indicator. The consumer or analyst must consider the purpose of the indicator and then make an educated and reasoned judgment about the substantive significance of the differences that are present in the indicator.

Trend Analysis and Change

The concept of time is a critical element to many indicator systems. The current status of a particular topic is often compared to its status at a previous point in time to assess how things have changed over time. Such over-time comparisons are often very informative and provide valuable information for describing changes in a particular educational topic or problem. It seems straightforward to compare an indicator over time, and oftentimes it is a rather simple exercise to perform such a comparison. However, there can also be factors that complicate the execution of an over-time comparison. One of the most common complications—one that we explore here—is a changing composition of the population of interest.

To illustrate how the changing composition of a population can affect the interpretation of an indicator, consider the findings from the NAEP reading long-term trend assessment presented in Figure 4.4. The average NAEP scale score for all groups of 17-year-olds was unchanged from 1975 to 2008. On the surface this looks like bad news. Clearly, we hope that stu-

Figure 4.4. Long-term trend NAEP reading scores, by race/ethnicity: 1975 and 2008

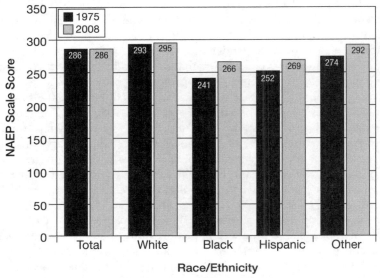

Note. The NAEP Long-Term Trend Reading scale ranges from 0 to 500.

Source. U.S. Department of Education, Institute of Education Sciences, National Center for Education Statistics, National Assessment of Educational Progress (NAEP), 1975 and 2008 Long-Term Trend Reading Assessments.

dent achievement improves over time. However, if we examine the indicator with a bit more scrutiny, we uncover some factors that complicate the interpretation of a seemingly straightforward finding that reading achievement among 17-year-olds has remained flat over time.

When we take a closer look at the NAEP scores that are disaggregated by race/ethnicity, we see that since 1975 all race/ethnic groups increased their reading performance. On the surface, it is a bit puzzling that all racial/ethnic subgroups have increased their performance, but the overall performance has remained unchanged. How can this be? The puzzling result relates directly to the changing testing population; the sample of students taking the NAEP assessment in 2008 contained a substantially larger proportion of Hispanics than it did in 1975. Specifically, in 1975 the sample of 17-year-olds that completed the NAEP reading assessment was 84% White, 11% Black, and 3% Hispanic. By 2008, the sample of 17-year-olds that completed the NAEP was 59% White, 15% Black, and 18% Hispanic. Clearly, the composition of the sample changed dramatically over this period of time. For a variety of reasons, Hispanic and Black students tend to score lower on the NAEP reading assessment. So although Black and Hispanic students have made larger gains than their White peers between 1975 and 2008, their average scores remain lower than the average for White students. Consequently, their increasing representation within the overall population has the effect of masking overall gains, even as each individual group within the population is improving. This is known as Simpson's Paradox and illustrates that over-time comparisons can provide very useful information, but that such comparisons can be more complex than they initially appear. Among all the other issues described in this book, consumers need to consider whether the composition of the population used in an over-time comparison has remained consistent over that time period. Rarely does this ever happen.

Inflation (Cost-of-Living) Adjustments

In addition to considering whether an indicator that performs an over-time comparison uses comparable populations, it is also important to assess whether an indicator that makes an over-time comparison uses a comparable unit of analysis. This issue mainly arises in the context of indicators that are based on dollars, such as expenditures, salaries, and revenues. With such indicators, it is important to assess whether the dollar values have been standardized to a common year, or "adjusted." Inflation adjustments, which are also referred to as cost-of-living adjustments, allow for useful comparisons over time by standardizing the dollar values to a given year, usually the most current or "today's dollars." The most common inflation adjustment is based on the Consumer Price Index (CPI), which is published by the U.S. Labor Department (NCES 2001-323). This index tracks the cost of some commonly purchased goods and services over time to create an adjustment factor.

To illustrate the importance of inflation adjustments, consider Figure 4.5. This figure shows the mean teacher salaries in four selected years in both unadjusted dollars (which the figure refers to as "current dollars") and adjusted dollars (which the figure refers to as "constant dollars"). In 1991, on average, teachers earned $31,300 compared to $44,400 in 2004. These salary estimates, which are not adjusted for inflation, make it appear that teacher salaries increased by 42% between 1990–91 and 2003–04. However, when salaries are adjusted for inflation and expressed in 2006 dollars, we see that in 1991 teachers earned, on average, the equivalent of $47,800. In 2004, the average teacher salary was $48,700. After controlling for inflation, mean teacher salaries only increased 2% between 1990–91 and 2003–

Figure 4.5. Teacher salaries in current and constant dollars: 1991–2004

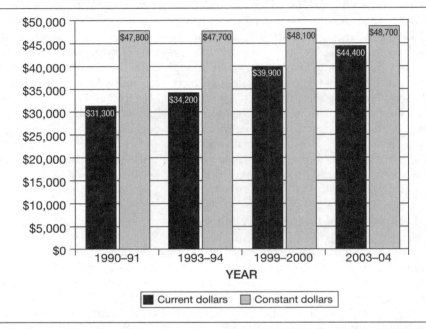

Source. U.S. Department of Education, National Center for Education Statistics, Schools and Staffing Survey (SASS), "Public Teacher Questionnaire," 1990–91, 1993–94, 1999–2000, 2003–04; and "Charter Teacher Questionnaire," 1999–2000.

04. Clearly, the choice of whether to control for inflation has a large impact on the substantive conclusions that can be drawn from the indicator.

Per Capita Adjustments

Earlier, we described how the changing composition of a population can affect over-time comparisons in indicators. A second factor that can affect indicators that present over-time comparisons is the consistency in the size of the population. This is especially applicable to indicators that present estimates of totals, whether it be total expenditures, total revenues, total criminal incidents, or any other topic. As an example, consider total public school expenditures in Table 4.11. Looking at the first column in the chart, which does not adjust the expenditures for inflation, we see that total expenditures have increased from $213 billion in 1989–90 to $528 billion in 2005–06, which is an increase of 149%. When we adjust the expenditures

Table 4.11. Total public school expenditures

Year	Total Expenditure, Current Dollars (in millions)	Total Expenditure, Constant Dollars (in millions)	Total Expenditure, Constant Dollars Per Pupil	Number of Pupils (in thousands)
1989–90	212,770	342,070	8,319	41,217
2005–06	528,735	542,408	10,889	49,299
% change	**149**	**59**	**31**	**20**

Source. U.S. Department of Education, National Center for Education Statistics, Common Core of Data (CCD), "National Public Education Financial Survey," 1987–88 through 2005–06.

to 2005–06 dollars to account for inflation we see a less dramatic increase of 59%. This again demonstrates how inflation adjustments can alter the conclusions drawn from an indicator.

Accounting for inflation answers the question of how expenditures have increased in constant dollars, but it might also be interesting to know how much of the increase is simply due to an increase in the number of students attending public schools. Between 1990 and 2006 public school enrollment increased by about 20%, from 41 million students to 49 million. To examine how much expenditures have increased due to factors unrelated to enrollment increases, we can measure expenditures as a per capita rate. For each year, we simply divide the total expenditures by the total enrollment. Now we show a 31% increase in the total expenditure per student over the past 15 years, increasing from $8,319 per student to $10,889 per student. This example illustrates how each measure provides a unique look at expenditures, and how multiple perspectives can provide a more comprehensive description of a topic.

Changes in Policy

A final factor to consider when examining an indicator that describes changes over time is the consistency of policies and programs. The estimates presented in an indicator may indicate true changes in a phenomenon, but such changes can also be a product of increased attention on a specific topic. Such attention may lead to increased perception of events or the implementation of formal procedures for recognizing and recording a specific event. For example, there has been a good deal of policy attention bestowed on issues of bullying in recent years. As a result, school administrators, students, and teachers have all been made much more aware of the issue of bullying. They have been taught to recognize these situations and to report them

Figure 4.6. Percentage of 3– to 21–year–olds in early education centers or public schools receiving services under the Individuals with Disabilities Education Act (IDEA), by primary disability type: 1976–77 to 2006–07

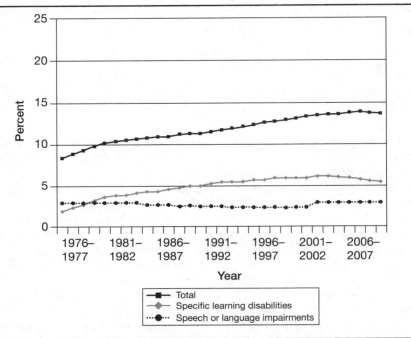

Source. U.S. Department of Education, Office of Special Education and Rehabilitative Services, *Annual Report to Congress on the Implementation of the Individuals with Disabilities Education Act*, selected years, 1977 through 2006, and Individuals with Disabilities Education Act (IDEA) database. Retrieved August 1, 2008, from http://www.ideadata.org/PartBdata.asp. U.S. Department of Education, National Center for Education Statistics, *Statistics of Public Elementary and Secondary School Systems, 1976–77 through 1980–81*, and Common Core of Data (CCD), "State Nonfiscal Survey of Public Elementary/Secondary Education," 1981–82 through 2006–07.

to formal networks. The changes in school bullying levels shown in many indicators may be a product of the reporting dynamics rather than any real increase in student bullying events.

Another recent example relates to the number of children with disabilities. Figure 4.6. shows the total number of children receiving special education services from 1976–77 to 2006–07. The number and percentage of students identified as having disabilities increased nearly every year between

1976–77 and 2005–06. The increase may actually be a product of more students with disabilities, but it could also be a product of schools identifying students with disabilities at greater rates because of increased policy attention that had been devoted to the issue. The increased attention may have resulted in the implementation of valid testing procedures to identify students with disabilities, the allocation of additional resources to serve kids with disabilities, or changes in the definitions of specific disabilities. These examples illustrate how changes in attention or policy can influence the estimates that are presented in indicators.

Finally, we must also be concerned with technical and administrative changes in data collection that might occur over time. For example, significant changes to how specific questions are asked or how the information is collected (in-person versus by phone) are very likely to cause quantitative and qualitative changes in the estimate that are not reflective of "true" changes in the population. When this type of administrative change is made in a data collection it is considered a "break-in-series" and readers are often cautioned about making conclusions about trends. In many cases, when a serious break-in-series occurs, time trends will not be reported out, and previous waves will be dropped from future publications.

Measuring Student Achievement

In many ways, standardized assessments are the bread and butter of education indicators, as well as research and policy. Assessing the abilities and knowledge of U.S. students is a critical performance indicator. This is now more apparent with the focus on testing since the passage of the No Child Left Behind Act of 2001. The law requires that each state establish assessment-based accountability systems to ensure that all students make adequately yearly progress toward proficiency in reading and mathematics:

> Each State shall establish a timeline for adequate yearly progress. The timeline shall ensure that not later than 12 years after the end of the 2001–2002 school year, all students in each group described in subparagraph (C)(v) will meet or exceed the State's proficient level of academic achievement on the State assessments under paragraph (3). (NCLB, 2002, Sec. 1111)

Typically, adequate yearly progress (AYP) is measured, in part, by the extent to which a student group demonstrates proficiency in the subject matter, as measured by a state-specific standardized assessment. The law identifies 10 student groups that must meet AYP levels: all students, students with disabilities, students with limited English proficiency, economically disadvantaged students, and each of six student racial/ethnic groups (African American/Black, Hispanic, Asian, White, Native American, and multiracial).

The rigors of the assessment requirements included in the NCLB legislation presented new challenges for assessing student achievement. States, districts, and schools have responded to these challenges by establishing new systems or reworking existing systems to meet the more rigorous requirements. The focus on standardized assessments has led to tremendous debate and controversy related to what should be tested, who should be tested, how the test findings are to be used, and potential unintended consequences associated with a reliance on standardized test formats to establish student proficiency. Volumes have been written about NCLB, and as a result we will not present a detailed review here.[3]

Instead of debating the merits of NCLB, our goal is to equip the reader to understand the basic language of assessments, the types of assessment typically used, and the issues related to the use of the assessment results. In many respects, the stages of assessment design mirror that of any other indicator. Beginning from conceptualization through measurement, the assessment design process must first develop a conceptual model as to what will be tested; work to create items or test questions that are concrete measures of these concepts; provide unbiased, valid, and reliable testing procedures; and process the data in a useful manner for the intended audience and purpose.

One useful way to think about assessments is as specialized surveys that attempt to gauge the ability of the respondent on a particular subject or topic. Assessments range from the 15-minute spelling test that everyone took in elementary school to the end-of-course Advanced Placement examinations, and for some, the college admissions SATs. Some states have adopted exit exams, such as end-of-course exams and high school graduation exams, that students must pass to demonstrate proficiency before moving on to the next subject or qualifying for a high school diploma (Warren & Kulick, 2007). While the assessments most relevant to education indicators are generally those administered to students, it should be noted that assessments can used to evaluate schools, teachers, and principals as well.[4] The theme tying these disparate types of assessments together is the fact that they are all designed to assess a person's ability on a particular subject.

There are several specific assessments that are routinely used to create education indicators, both national and international. The first of these assessments is the National Assessment of Educational Progress (NAEP), which is often called the "Nation's Report Card." NAEP is administered to a national sample of students in public and private elementary and secondary schools and is designed to measure student achievement across a broad range of subjects, including mathematics, reading, science, arts, history, economics, writing, and geography. NAEP allows for comparisons between states, and between states and the nation as a whole. NAEP, sponsored by the U.S. Department of Education, has been conducted since 1969 and is one of the most well-known assessments that paints a portrait of student achievement within the United States.

Other large-scale assessments that often serve as the basis for indicators include the Trends in International Mathematics and Science Study (TIMSS) and the Program for International Student Assessment (PISA). TIMSS, organized by the International Association for the Evaluation of Educational Achievement (IEA), is an assessment of student performance in mathematics and science in the fourth and eighth grades. Through participation in TIMSS, participating countries have access to reliable and valid data on student mathematics and science achievement around the world. PISA is organized by the Organization for Economic Cooperation and Development (OECD), an intergovernmental organization of industrialized countries. A system of international assessments that focus on 15-year-olds' capabilities in reading literacy, mathematics literacy, and science literacy, PISA emphasizes functional skills that students have acquired as they near the end of mandatory schooling.

While both TIMSS and PISA measure the mathematics and science achievement of students, they do this in somewhat different ways in different sets of countries for different sets of students. Consequently, the interpretation of the findings may be difficult to reconcile. First, TIMSS assesses fourth and eighth-graders, while PISA is an assessment of 15-year-old students, regardless of grade level. Second, the knowledge and skills measured in the two assessments differ. PISA is focused on application of knowledge to "real-world" situations, while TIMSS is intended to measure how well students have learned the mathematics and science curricula in participating countries. Third, the partner countries in the two assessments differ. Both assessments cover much of the world, but the overlap between them is not complete. PISA focuses principally on the 30 OECD-member nations, treating the non-OECD jurisdictions separately. TIMSS includes a larger proportion of developing countries and only about 25% of TIMSS countries also participate in PISA. The United States participates in both studies.

All assessments are designed to describe the achievement of a particular population within a specific subject area with a general purpose in mind. While it may seem that we are in the weeds with such nuances, these aspects are critical for understanding what any assessment measure is indicating. We now briefly review the different types of student assessments and assessment scores.

Types of Assessment

We can sort assessments into two general types: summative and formative. Summative examinations are those used by college entrance examinations, Advanced Placement courses, state testing, and the large-scale assessments such as NAEP, TIMSS, and PISA that we described above. *Summative assessments* are designed to evaluate what students have learned over a given period of time and the amount of knowledge or skills that they currently possess. These are comprehensive assessments of course content or subject area. Often considered high-stakes examinations, they are used to make decisions about student progress, acceptance into schools and programs, teacher and school quality, and a plethora of other outcomes. As a general rule, education indicators that rely on assessment data draw on summative assessments.

Formative assessments are designed as a diagnostic tool to provide feedback during the learning process (Boston, 2002; Sharkey & Murnane, 2006; Shepard, Hammerness, Darling-Hammond, & Rust, 2005). They are designed to provide real-time information on student progress in order to adjust classroom materials and curriculum, or to find out how students are processing information and coursework exercises. Adjustments can be made to meet student needs, and students gain an understanding about their performance, course expectations, and what they may need to do to succeed. Formative assessments are quite useful, but they are rarely used in the context of education indicators.

Assessments can also be organized by their design and use. Two general classes are norm-referenced and criterion-referenced tests (Bond, 1996). *Norm-referenced tests* relate a student's performance to other test takers in the population. Percentile rank is the most common metric used to report out norm-referenced tests. Schools use norm-referenced tests to classify students into particular programs (e.g., remedial or advanced placement) and are also used to place students into instructional groups or ability levels. In contrast, *criterion-referenced tests* are used to evaluate what a student knows against a particular benchmark, standard, or proficiency level. These scores are used to determine what a student knows. All students can do well or poorly on the exam.

There are many reasons why standardized assessments, in particular summative assessments, are not perfect indicators of student achievement (Bracey, 2002, 2006). We list seven of the more important reasons here: the test or testing process may be flawed in some way; a student's performance on any given day may or may not reflect his/her true ability; proficiency cut points are not aligned with adequate levels of student achievement; estimates based on small groups can be misleading; confusion between norm-referenced and criterion-referenced tests; confusion about the appropriate metrics; and problems associated with the testing process (e.g., changes or anomalies in the student sampling or selection criteria, changes in the test items, and changes in testing procedures). Each can have a significant impact on how we interpret and eventually act on findings from assessments. However, assessments are appealing from the point of view of indicator developers as they present a clear, concise way to summarize student achievement. When used correctly, assessments can provide a powerful method for describing the extent of knowledge and skills in a predefined population. One goal of this section of the chapter is to equip the reader with the skills to determine whether assessment results are being used in a manner that will provide an accurate and high-quality depiction of student achievement.

Types of Assessment Scores

The results of student assessments can be reported in a wide variety of manners. Raw test scores, scale scores, percentage correct, percentile ranking, grade equivalent, proficiency level, and growth model scores are all used to convey the results of assessments, and can indicate a student's relative position, what a student knows, and how much he or she has learned. We describe each of these scoring metrics in a bit more detail below.

The *raw score* is simply the number of items a student gets correct. If all tests were based on 100 questions, each worth one point, then the raw score would have some value. However, tests vary by the number of items and the degree of difficulty. If we do not know the number of items on the test, the number right is somewhat meaningless. Similarly, some tests are more difficult than others. In these cases, comparing the raw scores would not provide a fair comparison. However, if a group of students take identical exams, the raw score can provide a useful description of ability.

Many of the large-scale assessments—such as the NAEP, TIMSS, SAT, ACT, GRE, and many others—administer multiple versions of the assessment. Raw scores are converted to a *scale score* through complex statistical techniques. The scale onto which raw scores are converted is arbitrary; it is simply meant to ensure that proper (reliable and valid) comparisons can be made between test takers. For example, the SAT transforms raw scores onto a scale that ranges from 200 to 800. Similarly, raw NAEP scores on the reading and mathematics assessments are transformed onto a scale that ranges from 0 to 500. Again, there is no inherent meaning in a scale score; it just allows for the execution of valid and reliable comparisons between test takers.

The *percentage correct* is another common method for reporting assessment results, and is calculated as the number correct divided by the number of items on the test. That number is then multiplied by 100 to obtain the percentage correct. Calculating the percentage correct eliminates the problem of assessments having different numbers of items, but we still know relatively little about a student's ability from a metric of percentage correct. Is 70% correct on an assessment good or bad? If the assessment is very easy, answering only 70% of the items correctly is not very good. However, if the assessment is incredibly difficult, then answering 70% of the items correctly could be highly impressive. It is important to get a relative measure against a precisely defined group or against a specific standard. To get such a reference point, we need to turn to other methods of expressing the results of assessments.

Percentile ranking is a common metric for comparing the performance of a student to the performance of all other students in a defined group. For example, the SAT typically reports out a student's scale score as well as the state and national percentile rank to which the scale score corresponds. In 2008 a scale score of 560 on the mathematics test was at the 64th percentile in the nation.[5] This means that a score of 560 was better than the scores of 64% of all individuals across the country who took the SAT in 2008. It is important to note that the relationships between scale scores and percentile rankings are not stable across test subjects. For example, in 2008, a scale score of 560 on the reading portion of the SAT put students at the 69th percentile nationally, compared to the 64th percentile on the mathematics portion.

Similarly, because the population of test takers changes from year to year, scale scores and percentile rankings may not be stable across years. For example, a scale score of 560 on the mathematics portion of the SAT that was at the 64th percentile nationally in 2008 was at the 63rd percentile in 2009. Again, it is important to remember that percentile rankings only indicate the performance of a test taker relative to all other test takers. They say nothing about the absolute level of knowledge or skills a test taker possesses. To determine if the student has achieved an advanced level of knowledge and ability in a particular subject area, standards-based metrics such as grade equivalent or proficiency levels are useful.

The *grade equivalent* is a number that is intended to describe where a student's achievement positions them in the standard K–12 system used in the United States. In grade equivalent scores, a decimal number is used to describe performance in terms of grade level and month. For example, if a fourth grader obtains a grade equivalent score of 5.3 on a mathematics test, this score is approximately equivalent to the average score of a student finishing the third month of fifth grade. Grade equivalents are often used in schools to measure a student's developmental level and growth from year to year.

Similarly, *proficiency levels* are benchmarks that are based on a cut point and denote a specific level of achievement. For example, NAEP has four proficiency levels—below basic, basic, proficient, and advanced—that it uses to describe levels of academic ability. These positions or levels are built onto a continuum ranging from the lowest to the highest level of achievement.

While proficiency levels are useful for conveying the absolute, if somewhat subjective, level of knowledge and skills possessed by a student, they also have some disadvantages. First, they can be a rather blunt method of conveying student achievement. A student at the bottom end of the proficiency range and a student at the top end of the range are both rated as "proficient," even though there is likely some difference, and perhaps a substantial difference, between the two students. Second, there is a somewhat arbitrary aspect to the setting of proficiency standards. A score or a set of skills that one person may rate as "proficient" may be considered to be lacking proficiency by a different person. While assessments attempt to mitigate this problem by assembling a group of experts to identify proficiency cut points, there is an undeniable subjective element to this exercise. Finally, proficiency scores (and many of the other metrics we discuss above) do little to isolate the contribution of schools to student learning. It is quite likely that some schools with a rather well-prepared student body (students from households with higher incomes, highly educated parents, formal preschool educational settings, and so on) add little to their growth, even though all students are "proficient." Likewise, a student body ill prepared for formal education may experience tremendous growth in their academic achievement, but the majority may still fall well below the proficiency benchmark. Having a static proficiency level tells us nothing about what they learn in school. To address this problem, some have called for measures that capture the growth between the beginning and end of the school year.

Value-added or *growth model scores* allow schools to identify gains (or declines) that student make in a given time period, usually a school year (Amrein-Beardsley, 2008; Andrejko, 2004; Braun, 2005; Reckase, 2004; Rubin, Stuart, & Zanutto, 2004). Ideally, schools would assemble annual scores for each year of education and assess learning in relation to the student's courses and teachers. These scores are seen as superior to relying on percentages or proficiency levels that describe student status but not how much they have learned. For example, in one class, all students can be at or above proficient, but experience very little learning during the school year. In contrast, another class may have only 50% of the students at or above proficient, but demonstrate significant gains throughout the school year.

Growth models, however, have come under intense scrutiny as more districts look to use student test scores as high-stakes evaluations of teachers and schools. The most significant issue relates to the fact that students are not randomly assigned to teachers. Students come in with a variety of cognitive and noncognitive characteristics that will affect test scores. Students vary by their current academic abilities, motivation, extracurricular activities, behavioral problems, parental support, and many other factors that affect learning. In addition, student progress is influenced by school environment, resources, and policies. Certainly all of these factors will come to bear on the amount a student learns each year. The challenge to a fair assessment of teacher effectiveness is the ability to account for these student and school variables.

In sum, all test scores, no matter which type they are or which test they are from, are subject to misinterpretation and misuse. All have limitations or weaknesses that are exaggerated through improper score use. The key is to choose the type of score that will most appropriately allow you to accomplish your purposes for testing. For example, grade equivalents are particularly suited to estimating a student's developmental status or year-to-year growth. They are particularly ill suited to identifying a student's standing within a group or diagnosing areas of relative strength and weakness.

GRAPHICS

An indicator is only useful if it is able to convey information about the topic it purports to describe in a clear and meaningful manner. Tables, figures, and graphs are often effective tools in summarizing patterns and relationships with descriptive statistics (Gelman, Pasarica, & Dodhai, 2002; Grenville & Macfarlane, 1988; Tufte, 2001; Wainer, 1984, 2008). These visual presentations allow the reader to grasp patterns and relationships quickly. However, graphics are only as good as the data that underlie them. In addition, displaying data effectively and accurately takes an understanding of how the information was collected and for what purpose. While every tabular or graphical presentation has its own unique characteristics, there are a number of fundamental rules or techniques that can result in clear, meaningful presentations. In general, researchers examining the use of tables and figures to convey ideas[6] find "tables are best suited for looking up specific information, and graphs are better for perceiving trends and making comparison" (Gelman, Pasarica, & Dodhia, 2002, p. 121).

Tables are perhaps the most common way to summarize important data for the reader. Wainer (1992) outlines three rules for constructing tables: (1) Organize the rows and columns in a manner that makes sense to the purpose of the table and to the reader. People read from left to right, so organize the information in that manner. For trend data, organizing by time is a must. (2) Rounding is critical in tables. We never want to show more detail than we can reliably justify, and it doesn't make any sense to show certain estimates beyond a single decimal place. Not many people would care or find useful a state high school graduation rate that was presented as 75.23356%. Certainly 75.2% or even 75% works just fine. This is also true with the size of the estimate you are using, regardless of reliability. For example, there is little value in reporting out average teacher salaries to the penny. Substantively, it serves little purpose to know that one group makes $1 or $2 more than another group. This type of detail serves only as visual noise to the reader. Rounding to the nearest $10 or $100 is likely to highlight groups that have substantive differences and not just any difference. (3) Use summary totals for rows and columns. These totals allow for comparisons to the total group norm. Additional factors that help to aid in the accurate communication of a table's purpose are having clear titles and column and row labels, and clearly stating the metric or unit used in the table body. Often tables will have multiple metrics. A neatly organized and properly labeled table, while seemingly obvious, can be challenging to generate. Keeping the purpose of the table simple helps to limit these issues.

Tables, however, can be challenging to digest even for the seasoned researcher. Graphical displays are often very effective ways for summarizing data differences between groups and over time. They can be very convincing in demonstrating associations between variables or in describing change over time. To avoid the pitfalls of bad graphical displays researchers should maintain consistent scales and proportions, emphasize meaningful differences, and eliminate chart clutter (Wainer, 1984, 2005).

Graph scales are easy to distort, by mistake or otherwise, and the reader should be in tune with these features immediately. The choice of the proper graph scale, along with the range and spacing, should be logical and determined by the units. For example, for the NAEP mathematics scores presented in Figure 4.3, it is important to show differences on a range that is meaningful. We could have easily restricted the NAEP range for gender differences to 260–285 points on the 500-point NAEP scale. However, this would have had the affect of highlighting meaningless differences between males and females. Likewise, we would not want to use a scale that hides important differences or frames the indicator on unnecessarily wide ranges. For example, it would not be meaningful to show teacher salaries on a range from $0–$1,000,000. One million dollars, or for that matter $0, is not a common or useful end point for a national average of about $50,000.

For indicators, the use of tables and graphs are a necessary, if not preferred, way to summarize important findings. They can quickly and effectively convey the appropriate relationship and significance of a relationship when properly constructed. Tables and graphs, however, are only a means of presenting data and are only as good as the quality of the data.

CHAPTER 5

The Misuse of
Statistical Indicators

Not everything that counts can be counted, and not everything that can be counted counts.

—*Albert Einstein*

Statistics are like a bikini. What they reveal is suggestive, but what they conceal is vital.

—*Aaron Levenstein*

The previous chapters have identified and described in substantial detail several factors that can affect the overall quality of an indicator. Chapter 2 focused on issues of measurement and described the important role that measurement can play in determining the reliability and validity of an indicator; it also discussed how reliability and validity can affect the quality of an indicator. Chapter 3 briefly outlined the data collection process and then focused on various types of error that can enter into indicators, specifically sampling error and several types of nonsampling error. Chapter 4 described how the quality of an indicator can be affected by issues associated with the analysis and presentation of data, outlining the various metrics that indicators routinely use to present information, addressing issues specific to assessments, and discussing the graphical presentation of information.

With all of these potential problems that can afflict an indicator, the construction of a perfect indicator seems impossible. Chapter 2 illustrated that we can never measure what we intend to measure with perfection; there is always some inconsistency in how we measure a concept. Similarly, we rarely have a perfect match between our target population and our sampling frame. Chapter 3 detailed how error can seep into the data collection process. Chapter 4 demonstrated how different analytical decisions and techniques can alter the substantive conclusions that are drawn. Constraints associated with funding and time prevent the analyst from performing every possible analysis. As a result, the information presented in an indicator is only as good as the individual who produced the analysis.

Throughout this book we have stressed that indicators will never be perfect, and consumers of indicators need to assess the extent to which the indicator deviates from the "ideal" process. Most important, we must determine whether the deviations introduce significant and important error. We must first assess the error structure and then determine, for a given purpose, whether the error is in an acceptable range for us to decide with a certain level of confidence that the indicator reflects reality. Ultimately this error structure—the quantity and quality of error introduced through the selection, measurement, and dissemination process—is the measure of the estimate's quality.

MANIPULATION OF INDICATORS

There are many times when it is nearly impossible to understand an indicator's quality because the necessary information is not available or easily understandable. Whether intentional or not, statistics are often misinterpreted, distorted, or just plain wrong. In a commentary on the methodological challenges associated with the assessment of social policy, Donald Campbell (1976) notes, "The more any quantitative social indicator is used for social decision making, the more subject it will be to corruption pressures and the more apt it will be to distort and corrupt the social processes it is intended to monitor." Referred to as Campbell's Law, this statement implies that most indicators are subject to "political system problems." Once measures are used to inform policy or assess performance, these metrics are prone to manipulation, gaming, and distortion without proper oversight and accountability. The result may affect not only the indicator, but also the actual social process it is intended to measure. There becomes a perverse incentive to maximize the positive side of an indicator often at the cost of program's goals and intended purpose.

The problem of indicator corruptability is certainly not exclusive to the field of education, or for that matter, the social sciences (Best, 2001; Crossen, 1994; Gigerenzer et al., 2008; Hewitt, 1996; Kondratas, 1991). Nevertheless, there are some interesting examples from the field of education. For example, if a school demonstrated increases in annual average mathematics and reading test scores, this is often a cause for excitement and praise. However, it could be the case that the test score gains were due in part to increases in school dropouts; that is, if low-performing students dropped out of school, leaving only relatively higher-achieving students in school who produce higher test scores, there may be less excitement over the higher test scores. The focus solely on maximizing test score performance indicators may adversely affect the primary goal of our educational system, which is presumably to educate the entire community's adolescent population and not just a select portion.

Similarly, in the 1980s and 1990s there was a movement to increase the number of credits students had to earn, especially in math and science, in order to be allowed to graduate from high school. As a result, there was a large focus placed on the topic of student course-taking and indicators were developed to measure this topic. The course-taking reforms were designed to increase the number of advanced math and science courses taken by students, but there is some evidence that students were meeting the higher requirements not through the completion of advanced coursework, but by other means such as the completion of electives that were generously classified as math and science coursework. Again, this is an example of a situation where the focus of using indicators to monitor performance or compliance can lead to a situation where compliance is achieved with the letter of the law, but not with the spirit of the law. Indicators are good at measuring adherence to the letter of a law or policy. They are less effective at measuring compliance with its spirit.

USING INDICATORS TO ADVANCE AN INTEREST

Since Darrell Huff's classic work titled *How to Lie with Statistics* (1954), contemporary writers such as Joel Best (2001) and Cynthia Crossen (1994) have emerged to expose glaring examples of distorted statistics in a variety of social problems. The generation of suspicious data has been notably highlighted in what has become referred to as advocacy research. *Advocacy research* is defined as "studies that seek to measure social problems, heighten public awareness of them, and recommend possible solutions" (Gilbert, 1997, p. 101). Advocacy research has been traced to the early 1900s and has become a mainstream part of contemporary research and publishing. However, for some, it has diverged from its early standards of quality scholarship and progressed into one of questionable estimates and issue distortion. The reason is largely due to the very high stakes in today's policy environment (Campbell, 1976; Etzioni, 1968; Gilbert, 1997; Nichols & Berliner, 2007). Millions, even billions, of dollars are available to fund worthwhile issues, and advocates may feel the need to use numbers and indicators to demonstrate the importance of their pet issue. Similarly, indicators can be used to urge policy makers to consider a particular issue or to prompt more research and investigation into a particular issue or problem. There are certainly respectable and scientific examples of indicators being used to shine a light on serious social problems. The problem occurs when indicators are used to overstate the magnitude of the problem, clouding the issue with statistics based on dubious data sources, questionable definitions, generous assumptions, or sloppy calculations.

The most common method of using indicators to focus attention on an issue involves publishing numbers that are substantively large and immediately grab attention. These numbers are often released from sources that are perceived to be an authority or to have scientific legitimacy. From the perspective of an advocate, the importance of producing large numbers cannot be overstated. Large numbers tell us that a problem or topic is ubiquitous, affecting enough people and places to warrant concern among policy makers and the general public. It is a critical selling point. Very often the estimate has been generated from (1) a very broad, and thus meaningless definition (referred to as "widening the net"); (2) based on unreliable samples (national estimates built on a very small number of cases); or (3) select, unrepresentative nonprobability samples that do not generalize to the larger populations.[1]

Max Singer's (1971) seminal piece, "The Vitality of Mythical Numbers," dissects the process of generating inflated numbers and their promotion through different members of the media. Examining the assertion that NYC heroin addicts steal between 2 to 5 billion dollars of property each year, he finds no evidence to substantiate these claims, and his best guess is one tenth the size. He makes this conclusion:

> [This] exercise is another reminder that even responsible officials, responsible newspapers, and responsible research groups pick up and pass on as gospel numbers that have no real basis in fact. We are reminded by this experience that because an estimate has been used widely by a variety of people who should know what they are talking about, one cannot assume that the estimate is even approximately correct. (p. 6)

Peter Reuter (1984) followed up on Singer's work 13 years later and raised new concerns about the lack of progress in society's ability to detect dubious statistics. His concerns were more targeted toward the government's role in the production of highly implausible estimates. In fact, he suggests that "behind the complex estimating formula is some very questionable, but unquestioned, data collection. There is a strong interest in keeping the number high and none in keeping it correct. In that respect the estimated number...is one of a class of 'mythical numbers' that is becoming the routine product of government agencies. These numbers are generated by the demand that the government appear to know a great deal more than it actually does" (p. 136). Reuter summarizes that such numbers are allowed to circulate without criticism when three conditions are met: First, numbers are likely to be inflated when no constituency exists for keeping the numbers accurate, but a large constituency exists for keeping them high.

High numbers establish the "immensity of the existing problem." Second, unreasonably high estimates are likely to exist when there is a "lack of any systematic scholarly interest in the whole issue." The assumption underlying this condition is that scholars will impose outside scrutiny, which will keep the numbers within a realistic range. Third, estimates are most likely to be overestimated when they "have almost no policy consequences." If, for example, budgets were directly linked to estimates, they would certainly invite closer scrutiny.

We would propose a fourth condition to Reuter's list: statistical illiteracy. Once these "emotive statistics" or factoids catch on, they can be very persistent and difficult to correct or put in the proper context because it is not completely understood how they were generated. The problem is exacerbated by the 24-7 media cycle, where journalists are always on the lookout for the next big news story and not overly interested in the process that was used to produce the estimates they are presenting. Journalists, policy makers, and the public contribute to the proliferation of bad statistics. And it is not just indicators that are problematic. Compelling research findings have a knack for hanging around for similar reasons. Jeremy Freese (2008) makes the following observation:

> Part of what makes the . . . hypothesis perhaps more "vampirical" than "empirical"—unable to be killed by mere evidence—is that the hypothesis seems so logically compelling that it becomes easy to presume that it must be true, and to presume that the . . . literature on the hypothesis is an unproblematic avalanche of supporting findings. (p. 25)

In education Gerald Bracey and David Berliner are some of the more well-known researchers who have questioned the litany of numbers thrown around in education research and policy. Bracey has written such works as *Education Hell: Rhetoric vs. Reality* (2009), *Reading Educational Research: How to Avoid Getting Statistically Snookered* (2006) and *Setting the Record Straight: Responses to Misconceptions About Public Education in the U.S.* (2004). Berliner has produced such works as *Manufactured Crisis* (Berliner & Biddle, 1996) and *Collateral Damage: How High-Stakes Testing Corrupts America's Schools* (Nichols & Berliner, 2007). These books outline the negative consequences that occur when schools rely on poorly conceived metrics, indicators, and research. They present examples of what can happen when researchers deviate too far from acceptable operating practices or fail to disclose important and significant sources of error associated with a particular measure.

Many examples stem from simple misinterpretations or miscommunications on the part of the authors or audience; these are not deliberate. In some cases they are distortions of what was actually published. No matter how many caveats or limitations are presented in any indicator, one cannot assume the audience will take these into consideration or fully understand the caveats in their proper context. Other types of statistical problems fall into the category of strategic actions by school officials, researchers, or policy wonks to manipulate outcomes or perceptions. Such examples include outright cheating on tests where students are given answers or other types of improper aid or where tests and answers are altered by administrators (Nichols & Berliner, 2007). Such examples underscore the importance of indicator quality, transparency, and accountability. Knowing how the indicators were generated is just as critical as to knowing what the indicators say.

SO WHAT CAN BE DONE?

Throughout this book, we have stressed that an indicator will always have imperfections and errors, and the key to the use of an indicator is to assess whether it is of sufficient quality for the purpose at hand. Groves and Couper (2001) perhaps sum up this sentiment and line of reasoning best:

> As survey methodology, the study of how alternative survey designs affect the quality of statistics, matures, it is increasingly obvious that errors are only partially avoidable in surveys of human populations. Instead of having the goal of eliminating errors, survey researchers must learn how to reduce them within reason and budget and then attempt to gain insight into their impacts on key statistics in the survey. (p. 13)

By alerting readers to concepts such as validity and reliability, common sources of error, and the importance of statistical analysis and presentation, we have attempted to provide a framework for thinking about these imperfections and how they relate to the overall quality of an indicator. In short, we have described how every indicator—indeed, every statistic presented in an indicator—is a product of a string of important choices. These choices will result in an estimate, and based on the quality of the choices used to create the estimate, it may or may not be appropriate for the situation at hand. Within this estimation process, each indicator has error, and understanding the error structure is critical to understanding the substantive value of any indicator. While it is impossible to know all sources of error associated with an indicator, there are some fundamental questions any reader can ask to evaluate the error structure. Below, we present three groups of questions that individuals can ask and factors they can consider when attempting to evaluate the quality of an indicator.

1. How valid are the operational definitions and measures used in the construction of the indicator?
   a. When determining the validity, consider issues of face validity, content validity, criterion validity, construct validity, external validity, and statistical validity.
2. Are the measures used to generate the estimates presented in the indicator reliable?
   a. Is test-retest reliability a consideration that needs to be considered?
   b. What about interrater reliability?
3. If the operational definitions and measures used in the indicator are not perfectly valid or reliable, how extreme are the violations and how much will they affect the quality of the estimates presented in the indicator?
   a. The answer to this question is subjective in nature and depends to a large extent on the context and purpose for which the indicator is being used by the consumer.

EVALUATION QUESTIONS BASED ON CHAPTER 3

1. If the indicator is based on data collected using a sample:
   a. Was the sample selected in a random manner? That is, was it a probability selected sample?
      (1)   If not, do issues of external validity come into play?
   b. Are proper standard errors or margin of errors reported with each estimate?
      (1)   If not, is there any way to judge the reliability of the estimates?
   c. If standard errors are presented, are they sufficiently small to allow for confidence in the estimates?
      (1)   If standard errors are large, the estimates lack estimate precision.
   d. Were the data collected using a complex sampling design?
   e. If so, were estimates weighted properly to produce unbiased estimates for the target population?
      (1)   Presenting unweighted data can result in bias and incorrect estimates.
2. If the indicator is based on data collected using either a sample or universe:
   a. What is the population of interest?

(1)   Is it important for us to know something about this
        population?
(2)   Is the sampling frame representative of the population
        of interest?
b. Given the sampling frame, are there coverage problems?
    (1)   If significant parts of the population are not included
          in the sampling frame, bias will be introduced.
c. What are the unit response rates?
    (1)   Low response rates may indicate bias.
d. How was the question asked? For assessments, one should
    examine the item content and coverage with the intended
    framework (for example, does a mathematics assessment
    properly cover the course curriculum it is intended to
    measure?).
e. How was the information collected? Does the data collection
    mode present certain problems?
f. From whom were the data collected?
    (1)   Was this the most logical source from which to collect
          the data?
    (2)   How might source error enter the picture?
g. Is item nonresponse significant?
    (1)   High levels of item nonresponse can introduce bias.
h. How was the information coded and processed?

EVALUATION QUESTIONS BASED ON CHAPTER 4

1. What metric or metrics were used to present the information in
    the indicator?
    a. Does this metric have the ability to provide us with the
        information we want to know?
    b. Would alternative metrics have been more appropriate?
2. Does the indicator present evidence of statistically significant
    differences between groups of interest?
3. If there are statistically significant differences, are the differences
    substantively meaningful?
4. Does the indicator purport to examine trends over time? If so,
    consider the following factors:
    a. Are the populations at each time point comparable?
    b. If applicable, were the estimates adjusted for inflation or
        cost-of-living differences?
    c. If applicable, were per capita adjustments made?
    d. Could changes in the estimates over time be attributable to

    any important policy changes that occurred during the time
    period being analyzed?

5. Does the indicator use standardized assessment data to describe
   student achievement?

   a. If so, how are the achievement scores presented? Does this
      measure provide us with a relative picture of achievement
      or does it provide us with a picture of the absolute level of
      ability and skills that students possess?

   b. Would an alternative measure be preferable?

6. How is the information contained in the indicator presented?

   a. If it is presented in a tabular format, is the table organized in
      such a manner that you are able to interpret the results with
      confidence?

   b. If the information is presented graphically, is the scale
      meaningful and can any trends or meaningful group
      differences be identified with confidence?

These questions provide a solid starting point for evaluating the quality
of an indicator, but there are dozens of additional questions that could be
asked and issues that could be raised. However, the issues addressed in the
previous chapters of this book do represent the most important and common
threats to indicator quality.

We should note that successful evaluation of an indicator is dependent
upon the premise that researchers will routinely supply the paradata and information needed for a proper evaluation. In most cases it is possible to find
a summary of the basic measures of data quality. This is especially true with
large-scale national data generated by government agencies. At a minimum,
most reports describe the basic collection design and sample composition.
Others go farther and provide almost all of the information necessary to
make an informed assessment about the quality of an indicator.

The overall goal of this book is to provide readers with a framework and
tools for understanding and evaluating the quality and value of education
indicators. We have provided readers with an overview of the determinants
of quality by describing how indicators are generated and used in education.
In addition, we have provided real-world examples to illustrate our points
whenever we could. The seemingly straightforward process of indicator creation and development is, in actuality, rather complex, but it is our hope that
this complexity has become a bit more transparent and that the reader gains
an appreciation for the value and limitations associated with construction of
education indicators.

Notes

Chapter 1

1. First attributed to Leonard Henry Courtney (1895): "After all, facts are facts, and although we may quote one to another with a chuckle the words of the Wise Statesman, 'Lies—damned lies—and statistics,' still there are some easy figures the simplest must understand, and the astutest cannot wriggle out of."

2. This quote, commonly attributed to Wells, is actually a paraphrase by Samuel S. Wilks (1951) of the following sentence in *Mankind in the Making* (1904, p. 192): "The great body of physical science, a great deal of the essential fact of financial science, and endless social and political problems are only accessible and only thinkable to those who have had a sound training in mathematical analysis, and the time may not be very remote when it will be understood that for complete initiation as an efficient citizen . . . it is as necessary to be able to compute, to think in averages and maxima, as it is now to be able to read and write."

Chapter 2

1. The Classification of Secondary School Courses (CSSC) provides a general inventory of courses taught nationwide at the secondary school level—grades 9 through 12 (NCES, n.d.).

2. The research associated with official and administrative records related to crime is well-documented. For example, see Pridemore (2005) and Wiersema, Loftin, and McDowall (2000) for discrepancies in official measures of homicide, a seemingly straightforward counting process.

3. On dropout statistics: "One, anyone really familiar with education statistics knows dropout statistics are a mess, in part because jurisdictions have every incentive to under-report dropouts and over-report attendance. In most jurisdictions, school district revenues come from the state based directly, and often entirely, on the number of students the district claims to be teaching" (Phelps, 2005, p. 3).

4. For example, many burglary victims will say they got "robbed," but unlike burglary, robbery involves the direct contact or taking of property by force from another individual. More refined distinctions such as the difference between simple and aggravated assaults are even more problematic.

5. This is "indicator 27: School Crimes and Safety" in Planty et al. (2009). This indicator is also accessed directly at   http://nces.ed.gov/programs/coe/2009/pdf/27_2009.pdf

6. This indicator report can be found in Planty and DeVoe (2005). Appendix C (pp. 61–68) contains the specific instructions for the interviewer as well as the data collection instrument that the interviewer was required to fill out. It is interesting to note that interviewers were instructed to assess the facilities at the same time of day across all of the schools. This instruction was undoubtedly designed to maximize the validity of the assessments of the conditions of school facilities.

Chapter 3

1. This mention of universe surveys provides us with an opportunity to clarify a common source of confusion that often arises between samples and surveys. Many people use *survey* interchangeably with *sample,* but this is technically inaccurate. A survey is generally defined as a systematic collection of information, usually quantitative information. A survey may be from a sample or from the universe.

2. The Common Core of Data (CCD) is a universe collection of public schools and the Private School Survey is a universe collection of private schools in the United States. Both are collected by NCES (available online at http://nces.gov/ccd/ and http://nces.ed.gov/).

3. *Strata* are simply the groups formed from all possible combinations using the stratifying variables. For example, if you stratify by the 3 locale codes (rural, suburban, city) and 2 sector types (public, private) you end up with six stratum (public urban, public suburban, public rural, private urban, private suburban, and private rural).

4. A common concern with response rates deals with how much nonresponse is acceptable. 90%? 85%? 50%? The answer is: whenever bias is introduced. The assumption that higher response rates are preferred is dependent on how much the propensity to respond is related to the outcome of interest. A sample with a 95% response rate may have more bias than one with only an 80% response rate. A detailed investigation should be performed (Groves, 2006).

5. However, the authors do note that while the level of volunteering is overestimated, nonresponse bias does not have a similar affect on the characteristics of volunteers. That is, regardless of the response rates, studies tend to reveal similar characteristics for those who volunteer.

6. Many states require students to take the ACT test or the state university system requires ACT scores rather than SAT scores for admission. In 2008, all public high school 11th graders in the states of Colorado, Illinois, Kentucky, Michigan, and Wyoming were tested with the ACT as required by each state.

Chapter 4

1. "Indicator 20: Status Dropout Rates" is in Planty et al. (2009). It may also be accessed directly at http://nces.ed.gov/programs/coe/2009/pdf/20_2009.pdf

2. More directly, it is the effective sample size that is important. In a simple random sample, the effective sample size is about the same as the actual sample size chosen. However, when sample members are clustered (e.g., students in schools or persons in households), the effective sample size is much smaller than the actual sample size. Sample designs that use a cluster design are less efficient than simple random samples in that all else being equal, estimates from clustered samples will have larger standard errors than one from a simple random sample.

3. The literature is awash with papers and books on the No Child Left Behind Act. Some examples include: Peterson & West, 2003; Meier & Wood, 2004; Sunderman, Kim, & Orfield, 2005; Hess & Petrilli, 2006; Abernathy, 2007; Cronin, Dahlin, Adkins, & Kingsbury, 2007; Koretz, 2008; Linn, 2008.

4. We often equate assessments with students and the focus here is generally on the student. However, it is important to note that assessments are also used to evaluate teachers, principals, and schools. For example, college graduates who are looking to change careers and become high school teachers take New York State's LAST/ATS-W (Liberal Arts and Sciences Test/Assessment of Teaching Skills-Written) to earn certification to teach in any of New York State's 704 public school districts.

5. The SAT website has detailed explanations of their scoring system at *SAT: Understanding Your Scores,* available at http://sat.collegeboard.com//scores/understanding-sat-scores

6. The form of research often involves randomly assigning tables and graphs with varying designs to respondents who then answer a battery of questions about the substantive aspects of the graph. The graphs where the respondents correctly interpreted the data as evidenced by their answers are considered superior designs.

Chapter 5

1. Gilbert (1997, pp. 123–124) expands this list of advocacy research strategies to include asserting validation with other select, noncomparable studies; using professional publications as a means for establishing credibility; highlighting the larger findings with the use of selected atypical anecdotal examples; changing methodology and data in response to criticism; and resorting to ad hominem arguments when all else fails.

References

Abernathy, S. (2007). *No Child Left Behind and the public schools*. Ann Arbor: University of Michigan Press.

Abraham, K., Helms, S., & Presser, S. (2009). How social processes distort measurement: The impact of survey nonresponse on estimates of volunteer work in the United States. *American Journal of Sociology, 114,* 1129–1165.

Adcock, R., & Collier, D. (2001). Measurement validity: A shared standard for qualitative and quantitative research. *American Political Science Review (APSR), 95,* 529–546.

Ahmed, S. (n.d.). *Statistics for policy makers*. Washington, DC: National Center for Education Statistics, U.S. Department of Education.

American Association of Community Colleges (AACC). (2010). *Community college trends and statistics*. Washington, DC: Author. Retrieved March 9, 2010, from http://www.aacc.nche.edu/AboutCC/Trends/Pages/default.aspx

Amrein-Beardsley, A. (2008). Methodological concerns about the education value-added assessment system. *Educational Researcher, 37,* 65–75.

Andrejko, L. (2004). Value-added assessment: A view from a practitioner. *Journal of Educational and Behavioral Statistics, 29,* 7–9.

Asher, H. (2004). *Polling and the public: What every citizen should know, sixth edition*. Washington, DC: Congressional Quarterly Press.

Babbie, E. (2005). *The practice of social research* (10th ed.). Belmont, CA: Wadsworth.

Bauer, R. (1966). *Social indicators*. Cambridge, MA: Massachusetts Institute of Technology Press.

Berliner, D., & Biddle, B. (1996). *Manufactured crisis: Myths, fraud, and the attack on America's public schools*. New York: Perseus Publishing.

Best, J. (2001). *Damned lies and statistics*. Berkeley: University of California Press.

Best, J. (2004). *More damned lies and statistics*. Berkeley: University of California Press.

Biemer, P., Groves, R., Lyberg, L., Mathiowetz, N., & Sudman, S. (Eds.). (1991). *Measurement errors in surveys*. New York: John Wiley.

Biemer, P., & Lyberg, L. (2003). *Introduction to survey quality*. Hoboken, NJ: John Wiley & Sons.

Blalock, H. (1979). The presidential address: Measurement and conceptualization problems: The major obstacle to integrating theory and research. *American Sociological Review, 44*(6), 881–894.

Blank, R. (1993). Developing a system of education indicators: Selecting, implementing, and reporting indicators. *Educational Evaluation and Policy Analysis, 11,* 65–80.

Black, D., Sanders, S., & Taylor, L. (2003). Measurement of higher education in the census and current population survey. *Journal of the American Statistical Association, 98,* 545–554.

Blumberg, S., & Luke, J. (2007). Coverage bias in traditional telephone surveys of low-income and young adults. *Public Opinion Quarterly, 71,* 734–749.

Blumberg, S., & Luke, J. (2009). *Wireless substitution: Early release of estimates from the National Health Interview Survey.* Atlanta, GA: National Center for Health Statistics.

Bollen, K. A. (1989). *Structural equations with latent variables.* New York: Wiley.

Bond, L. A. (1996). Norm- and criterion-referenced testing. *Practical Assessment, Research & Evaluation, 5.* Retrieved December 7, 2009 from http://PAREonline. net/getvn.asp?v=5&n=2.

Boston, C. (2002). The concept of formative assessment. *Practical Assessment, Research & Evaluation, 8.* Retrieved December 7, 2009 from http://PAREonline. net/getvn.asp?v=8&n=9.

Bracey, G. (2002). *Put to the test: An educator's and consumer's guide to standardized testing.* Bloomington, IN: Phi Delta Kappa Internacional.

Bracey, G. (2004). *Setting the record straight: Responses to misconceptions about public education in the U.S.* Portsmouth, NH: Heinemann.

Bracey, G. (2006). *Reading educational research: How to avoid getting statistically snookered.* Portsmouth, NH: Heinemann.

Bracey, G. (2009). *Education hell: Rhetoric vs. reality.* Princeton, NJ: Educational Research Service.

Bradburn, N., Sudman, S., & Associates. (1979). *Improving interviewing methods and questionnaire design.* San Francisco: Jossey-Bass.

Bradburn, N., & Sudman, S. (1988). *Polls and surveys: Understanding what they tell us.* San Francisco: Jossey-Bass.

Braun, H. (2005). *Using student progress to evaluate teachers: A primer on value-added models.* Princeton, NJ: Educational Testing Service.

Brick, J., Cahalan, M., Gray, L., & Severynse, J. (1994). *A study of selected non-sampling errors in the 1991 survey of recent college graduates* (Technical Report NCES 95-640). Washington, DC: National Center for Education Statistics, U.S. Department of Education.

Brennan, R. L. (Ed.). (2006). *Educational measurement* (4th ed.). Westport, CT: American Council on Education/Praeger.

Bryk, A., & Hermanson, K. (1993). Educational indicator systems: Observations on their structure, interpretation, and use. *Review of Research in Education, 19,* 451–484.

Campbell, D. (1976). *Assessing the impact of planned social change.* (Occasional Paper No. 8). Hanover, NH: Dartmouth College. (ED303512)

Carmines, E., & Zeller, R. (1991). *Reliability and validity assessment.* Newbury Park, CA: Sage.

Center for Educational Reform (CER). (2009). Charter school laws across the states. Washington, DC: Author. Retrieved March 9, 2010, from http://www.edreform.

com/About_CER/Charter_School_Laws_Across_the_States/index.cfm

Converse, J., & Presser, S. (1989). *Survey questions: Handcrafting the standardized questionnaire.* Newbury Park, CA: Sage.

Council of Chief State School Officers (CCSSO). (n.d.) State education indicators. Washington, DC: Author. Retrieved March 9, 2010, from http://www.ccsso.org/Projects/State_Education_Indicators/

Cook, T. D. & Campbell, D. T. (1979). *Quasi-experimentation: Design and analysis issues for field settings.* Boston, MA: Houghton Mifflin Company.

Couper, M., & Lyberg, L. (2005). The use of paradata in survey research. In *Proceedings of the 55th Session of the International Statistical Institute*, Sydney, Australia.

Courtney, L. H. (1895). To my fellow-disciples at Saratoga Springs. *The National Review* (London), 26, 21–26;

Cronin, J., Dahlin, M., Adkins, D., & Kingsbury, G. G. (2007). *The proficiency illusion.* Washington, DC: Thomas Fordham Institute

Crossen, C. (1994). *Tainted truth: The manipulation of fact in America.* New York: Simon & Schuster.

Darling-Hammond, L. (1992). Educational indicators and enlightened policy. *Educational Policy, 6,* 235–265.

Darling-Hammond, L. (2000, January 1). Teacher quality and student achievement: A review of state policy evidence. *Education Policy Analysis Archives, 8.* Retrieved December 7, 2009, from http://epaa.asu.edu/epaa/v10n36.html

David, J. (1987). *Improving education with locally developed indicators* (CPRE Research Report RR-004). New Brunswick, NJ: State University of New Jersey, Center for Policy Research in Education.

David, J. (1988). The use of indicators by school districts: Aid or threat to improvement? *Phi Delta Kappan, 69,* 499–503.

Dee, T. (2005). A teacher like me: Does race, ethnicity, or gender matter? *American Economic Review, 95,* 158–165.

Ehrenberg, R., Goldhaber, D., & Brewer, D. (1995). Do teachers' race, gender and ethnicity matter? Evidence from the national educational longitudinal study of 1988. *Industrial and Labor Relations Review, 48*(3), 547–561.

Etzioni, A. (1968). Shortcuts to social change. *The Public Interest, 12,* 40–51.

Federal Committee on Statistical Methodology. (1978). *An error profile: Employment as measured by the current population survey.* Washington, DC: U.S. Office of Management and Budget (Statistical Policy Working Paper 3).

Federal Committee on Statistical Methodology. (1988). *Quality in establishment surveys.* Washington, DC: U.S. Office of Management and Budget (Statistical Policy Working Paper 15).

Federal Committee on Statistical Methodology. (1990). *Survey coverage.* Washington, DC: U.S. Office of Management and Budget (Statistical Policy Working Paper 17).

Figlio, D. (2006). Testing, crime, and punishment. *Journal of Public Economics 90,* 837–851.

Figlio, D., & Getzler, L. (2006). Accountability, ability, and disability: Gaming the system? In T. Gronberg & D. Cansen (Eds.), *Advances in microeconomics: Improving school accountability—check-ups or choice?* (Vol. 14, pp. 35–49). Amsterdam: Elsevier.

Fitz-Gibbon, C., & Tymms, P. (2002). Technical and ethical issues in indicator systems: Doing things right and doing wrong things. *Education Policy Analysis Archives* (Vol 10). Retrieved December 7, 2009, from http://epaa.asu.edu/epaa/v10n6/

Forte-Fast, E., & Hebbler, S. (2004). *A framework for examining validity in state accountability systems*. Washington, DC: Council of Chief State School Officers.

Fredericks, J., Blumenfeld, P., & Paris, A. (2004). School engagement: Potential of the concept, and state of the evidence. *Review of Educational Research, 74*(1), 59–109.

Freese, J. (2008). The problem of predictive promiscuity in deductive applications of evolutionary reasoning to intergenerational transfers: Three cautionary tales. In A. Booth, A. C. Crouter, S. Bianchi, & J. A. Seltzer (Eds.), *Caring and exchange within and across generations* (pp. 45–78). Washington, DC: Urban Institute Press.

Gelman, A., Pasarica, C., & Dodhia, R. (2002). Let's practice what we preach: Turning tables into graphs. *The American Statistician, 56,* 121–130.

Gigerenzer, G., Gaissmaier, W., Kurz-Milcke, E., Schwartz, L. M., & Woloshin, S. (2007). Helping doctors and patients to make sense of health statistics. *Psychological Science in the Public Interest, 8,* 53–96.

Gilbert, N. (1997). Advocacy research and social policy. In M. Tonry (Ed.), *Crime and justice: A review of research*. Chicago: University of Chicago Press.

Goldschmidt, P., & Choi, K. (2005). *Policy makers' guide to growth models and school accountability: How do accountability models differ?* Washington, DC: Council of Chief State School Officers.

Gonzalez, M., Ogus, J., Shapiro, G., & Tepping, B. (1975). Standards for discussion and presentation of errors in survey and census data. *Journal of the American Statistical Association, 70,* 351.

Grenville, S., & Macfarlane, I. (1988). Pitfalls of statistical presentation. In [Papers presented to the] *17th SEANZA Central Banking Course*. Sydney: Reserve Bank of Australia.

Groves, R. (1989). *Survey errors and survey costs*. New York: Wiley.

Groves, R. (2006). Nonresponse rates and nonresponse bias in household surveys. *Public Opinion Quarterly, 646–675.*

Groves, R., & Couper, M. (1998). *Nonresponse in household interview surveys*. New York: John Wiley.

Groves, R., & Couper, M. (2001). Designing surveys acknowledging nonresponse. In M. ver Ploeg, R. Moffitt, & C. Citro (Eds.), *Studies of welfare populations: Data collection and research issues* (pp. 11–54). Washington, DC: National Academy Press.

Groves, R., Fowler, F., Couper, M., Lepkowski, J., Singer, E., & Tourangeau, R. (2009). *Survey methodology* (2nd ed.). Hoboken, NJ: Wiley.

Guthrie, J. (1993). Do America's schools need a "Dow Jones index"? *Phi Delta Kappan, 4*(7), 523–528.

Hart, D., Donnelly, T., Youniss, J., & Atkins, R. (2007). High school community service as a predictor of adult voting and volunteering. *American Educational Research Journal, 44,* 197–219.

Hess, F. (2008). The new stupid. *Educational Leadership,* 1.

Hess, R., & Petrilli, M. (2006). *No child left behind*. New York: Peter Lang.

Hewitt, C. (2008). Estimating the number of homeless: Media misrepresentation of an urban problem. *Journal of Urban Affairs, 18,* 431–447.

Huff, D. (1954). *How to lie with statistics.* New York: Norton.

Hussar, W. J., & Bailey, T. M. (2009). *Projections of education statistics to 2018* (NCES 2009–062). Washington, DC: National Center for Education Statistics, Institute of Education Sciences, U.S. Department of Education.

Iezzoni, L. (1997). Assessing quality using administrative data. *Annals of Internal Medicine, 127,* 666–674.

Jaeger, R. (1978). About educational indicators: Statistics on the conditions and trends in education. *Review of Research in Education, 6,* 276–315.

Jaeger, R. (1990). *Statistics: A spectator sport.* Newbury Park, CA: Sage.

Kasprzyk, D., & Giesbrecht, L. (2003). Reporting sources of error in U.S. federal government surveys. *Journal of Official Statistics, 19.*

Kelman, S. (1985). Why should government gather statistics, anyway? *Journal of Official Statistics, 1,* 361–379.

King, G., Keohane, R., & Verba, S. (1994). *Designing social inquiry.* Princeton, NJ: Princeton University Press.

Kondratas, A. (1991). Estimates and public policy: The politics of numbers. *Housing Policy Debate, 2,* 631–647.

Koretz, D. (2008). *Measuring up: What educational testing really tells us.* Cambridge, MA: Harvard University Press.

Kuncel, N. R., Crede, M., & Thomas, L. L. (2005). The validity of self-reported grade point averages, class ranks, and test scores: A meta-analysis. *Review of Educational Research, 75,* 63–82.

Land, K. (1983). Social indicators. In R. H. Turner & J. F. Short (Eds.), *Annual Review of Sociology, 9,* 1–26. Palo Alto, CA: Annual Reviews.

Lauer, P. (2006). *An education research primer: How to understand, evaluate, and use it.* San Francisco, CA: Jossey-Bass.

Lessler, J., & Kalsbeek, W. (1992). *Nonsampling error in surveys.* New York: Wiley.

Levine, D. (1986). *Creating a center for education statistics: A time for action.* Washington, DC: National Academy Press.

Lewin, T. (2002, February 27). Teenage drinking a problem but not in way study found. *New York Times,* A19.

Linn, R. (2008). *Validation of uses and interpretations of state assessments.* Washington, DC: Council of Chief State School Officers.

Marion, S., White, C., Carlson, D., Erpenbach, W., Rabinowitz, S., & Sheinker, J. (2002). *Making valid and reliable decisions in determining adequate yearly progress.* Washington, DC: Council of Chief State School Officers.

Matheson, N., Salganik, L. H., Phelps, R. P., & Perie, M. (1996). *Education Indicators: An international perspective.* NCES 96-003, U.S. Department of Education, National Center for Education Statistics, Washington, D.C.

Mathews, J. (2007, December 27). Grading disparities peeve parents. *Washington Post,* p. A01.

McMillen-Seastrom, M., Gruber, K., Henke, R., McGrath, D. J., & Cohen, B. (2002). *Qualifications of the public school teacher workforce: Prevalence of out-of-field teaching 1987–88 to 1999–2000 (NCES 2002603).* Washington, DC: U.S. Department of Education, National Center for Education Statistics.

Meier, D., & Wood, G. (Eds.) (2004). *Many children left behind: How the No Child Left Behind Act is damaging our children and our schools.* Boston: Beacon Press.

Melnick, D. (2002). The legislative process and the use of indicators in formula allocations. *Journal of Official Statistics 18,* 353–369.

Mishel, L. (2006, March 7). The exaggerated dropout crisis. *Education Week.* Retrieved on April 10, 2010, from http://www.edweek.org/ew/articles/2006/03/08/26mishel.h25.html

Montgomery County Public Schools (MCPS). (2009). *School survey results.* Rockville, MD: Author. Retrieved March 9, 2010, from http://sharedaccountability.mcpsprimetime.org/SurveyResults/

Murnane, R. (1987). Improving education indicators and economic indicators: The same problem? *Educational Evaluation and Policy Analysis, 9,* 101–116.

National Center for Education Statistics. (1991). *Education counts: An indication system to monitor the nation's educational health* (NCES 91634). Washington, DC: Author.

National Center for Education Statistics (NCES). (2002). *Educational longitudinal study of 2002.* Washington, DC: Author. Available online at http://nces.ed.gov/surveys/ELS2002

National Center for Education Statistics (NCES). (2008). *Projections of education statistics to 2017* (NCES 2008-078). Washington, DC: Author. Retrieved March 9, 2010, from http://nces.ed.gov/programs/projections/projections2017

National Center for Education Statistics (NCES). (n.d.). High school transcript studies: SSC Courses/course codes. Washington, DC: Author. Retrieved March 9, 2010, from http://nces.ed.gov/surveys/hst/courses.asp

National Science Foundation. (NSF). (n.d.). *Science and engineering statistics.* Arlington, VA: Author. Retrieved March 9, 2010, from http://www.nsf.gov/statistics

National Survey of Student Engagement. (2009a). *Assessment for improvement: Tracking student engagement over time—annual results 2009.* Bloomington, IN: Indiana University Center for Postsecondary Research. Retrieved March 9, 2010, from http://nsse.iub.edu/NSSE_2009_Results/pdf/NSSE_AR_2009.pdf

National Survey of Student Engagement. (2009b). *NSSE 2009 overview.* Bloomington, IN: Indiana University Center for Postsecondary Research. Retrieved March 9, 2010, from http://nsse.iub.edu/2009_Institutional_Report/pdf/NSSE_2009_Overview.pdf

Nichols, S., & Berliner, D. (2007). *Collateral damage: How high-stakes testing corrupts America's schools.* Harvard University Press.

No Child Left Behind Act of 2001. Pub. L. No. 107-110, 115 Stat. 1425 (2002). Available online: http://www2.ed.gov.policy/elsec/leg/esea02/index/html

Oakes, J. (1986). *Educational indicators: A guide for policy makers.* Santa Monica, CA: Rand.

Oakes, J. (1989). What educational indicators? The case for assessing the school context. *Educational Evaluation and Policy Analysis, 11,* 181–199.

Odden, A. (1990). Educational indicators in the United States: The need for analysis. *Educational Researcher, 19,* 24–29.

Organisation for Economic Cooperation and Development (OECD). (2008). *Edu-*

cation at a glance 2008: OECD indicators. Paris: Author. Retrieved March 9, 2010, from http://www.oecd.org/edu/eag2008

Paulos, J. (1988). *Innumeracy: Mathematical illiteracy and its consequences.* New York: Hill and Wang.

Pedhazur, E. J., & Schmelkin, L. P. (1991). *Measurement, design, and analysis: An integrated approach.* Hillsdale, NJ: Erlbaum.

Peterson, P., & West, M. (2003). *No child left behind? The politics and practice of school accountability.* Washington, DC: Brookings Institution Press.

Phelps, R. (2005). A review of Greene (2002) High school graduation rates in the United States. *Practical Assessment, Research & Evaluation, 10*(15). Retrieved December 7, 2009, from http://pareonline.net/pdf/v10n15.pdf

Planty, M., & DeVoe, J. (2005). *An examination of the conditions of school facilities attended by 10th-grade students in 2002* (NCES 2006-302). Washington, DC: U.S. Department of Education, National Center for Education Statistics. Also available at http://nces.ed.gov/pubs2006/2006302.pdf

Planty, M. et al. (2008). *The condition of education 2008* (NCES 2008031). Washington, DC: U.S. Department of Education, National Center for Education Statistics.

Planty, M. et al. (2009). *The condition of education 2009* (NCES 2009081). Washington, DC: U.S. Department of Education, National Center for Education Statistics.

Porter, A. (1991). Creating a system of school process indicators. *Educational Evaluation and Policy Analysis, 13,* 13–29.

Powell, B., & Steelman, L. (1996). Bewitched, bothered, and bewildering: The use and misuse of state SAT and ACT scores. *Harvard Educational Review, 66,* 27–59.

Pridemore, W. (2005). A cautionary note on using county-level crime and homicide data. *Homicide Studies, 9,* 256–268.

Raudenbush, S. (2004). *Schooling, statistics, and poverty: Can we measure school improvement?* Princeton, NJ: Educational Testing System.

Reckase, M. (2004). The real world is more complicated than we would like. *Journal of Educational and Behavioral Statistics, 29,* 7–9.

Reuter, P. (1984). The (continued) vitality of mythical numbers. *Public Interest, 75,* 135–147.

Riley, K. A., & Nuttall, D. L. (Eds). (1994). *Measuring quality: Education indicators—United Kingdom and international perspectives.* London: Falmer.

Roy, J., & Mishel, L. (2008). Using administrative data to estimate graduation rates: Challenges, proposed solutions and their pitfalls. *Education Policy Analysis Archives 16,* 11. Retrieved April 20, 2010, from http://epaa.asu.edu/epaa/v16n11/

Rubin, D., Stuart, E., & Zanutto, E. (2004). A potential outcomes view of value-added assessment in education. *Journal of Educational and Behavioral Statistics, 29,* 103–116.

Salganik, L. (1994). Apples and apples: Comparing performance indicators for places with similar demographic characteristics. *Educational Evaluation and Policy Analysis, 16,* 125–141.

Salkind, N. (2007). *Statistics for people who (they think) hate statistics* (3rd ed.). Thousand Oaks, CA: Sage.

Salvucci, S., Walter, E., Conley, V., Fink, S., & Saba, M. (1997). *Measurement error studies at the National Center for Education Statistics* (NCES 2003-061). Washington, DC: U.S. Department of Education, National Center for Education Statistics.

Seastrom, M. (2002). *NCES statistical standards* (NCES 2003–061). Washington, DC: U.S. Department of Education, National Center for Education Statistics.

Selden, R. (1994). How indicators have been used in the USA. In K. A. Riley & D. L. Nuttall (Eds), *Measuring quality: Education indicators—United Kingdom and international perspectives* (pp. 41–68). London: Falmer.

Sharkey, N., & Murnane, R. (2006). Tough choices in designing a formative assessment system. *American Journal of Education, 112*(4), 572–588.

Shavelson, R., McDonnell, L., & Oakes, J. (1991). What are educational indicators and indicator systems? *Practical Assessment, Research & Evaluation*, Vol. 2. Retrieved December 7, 2009 from http://pareonline.net/getvn.asp?v=2&n=11

Shepard, L., Hammerness, K., Darling-Hammond, L., & Rust, F. (2005). Assessment. In L. Darling-Hammond & J. Bransford (Eds.), *Preparing teachers for a changing world: What teachers should learn and be able to do* (pp. 275–326). San Francisco: Jossey-Bass.

Singer, M. (1971). The vitality of mythical numbers. *The Public Interest, 23,* 3–9.

Skogan, W. (1974). The validity of official crime statistics: An empirical investigation. *Social Science Quarterly, 55,* 25–38.

Skogan, W. (1984). Reporting crimes to the police: The status of world research. *Journal of Research in Crime and Delinquency, 21,* 113–137.

Snyder, T. (Ed). (1993). *120 years of American education: A statistical portrait.* Washington, DC: National Center for Education Statistics.

Snyder, T. (2008). *The digest of education 2007.* Washington, DC: National Center for Education Statistics, U.S. Department of Education.

Stamp, J. (1929). *Some economic factors in modern life* (pp. 258–259). London: P.S. King & Son.

Stoneberg, B. (2005). Please don't use NAEP scores to rank order the 50 states. *Practical Assessment, Research & Evaluation, 10*(9). Retrieved December 7, 2009, from http://pareonline.net/getvn.asp?v=10&n=9

Sudman, S., & Bradburn, N. (1974). *Response effects in surveys: A review and synthesis.* Chicago: Aldine.

Sudman, S., Bradburn, N., & Schwarz, N. (1996). *Thinking about answers: The application of cognitive processes to survey methodology.* San Francisco: Jossey-Bass.

Sunderman, G., Kim, J., & Orfield, G. (2005). *NCLB meets school realities: Lessons from the field.* Thousand Oaks, CA: Corwin Press.

Tufte, E. (2001). *The visual display of quantitative information* (2nd ed.). Cheshire, CT: Graphics Press.

Turque, B. (2009, September 10). Enrollment in D.C. schools is close to target. *The Washington Post.* Retrieved Septmeber 17, 2009, from http://www.washingtonpost.com/wp-dyn/content/article/2009/09/09/AR2009090902230.html. Retrieved 9/17/09.

U.S. Census Bureau. (n.d.). *Current population survey.* Available online at http://www.census.gov/CPS/

Utts, J. (2003), What educated citizens should know about statistics and probability. *The American Statistician, 57,* 74–79.

Wainer, H. (1984). How to display data badly. *The American Statistician, 38,* 137–147.

Wainer, H. (1989). Eelworms, bullet holes, and Geraldine Ferraro: Some problems with statistical adjustment and some solutions. *Journal of Educational Statistics, 14,* 121–140.

Wainer, H. (1990). Commentary: Adjusting NAEP for self-selection: A useful place for "wall chart" technology? *Journal of Educational and Behavioral Statistics, 15,* 1–7.

Wainer, H. (1992). Understanding graphs and tables. *Educational Researcher, 21,* 14–23.

Wainer, H. (1993). Measurement problems. *Journal of Educational Measurement, 30,* 1–21.

Wainer, H. (2005). *Graphic discovery.* Princeton, NJ: Princeton University Press.

Wainer, H., Holland, P., Swinton, S., & Wang, M. (1985).On "state education statistics." *Journal of Educational Statistics, 10,* 293–325.

Warren, J., & Kulick, R. (2007). Modeling states' enactment of high school exit examination policies. *Social Forces, 86,* 215–230.

Wells, H. G. (1904). *Mankind in the making.* New York: Charles Scribner's Sons.

White Plisko, V., Ginsburg, A., & Chaikind, S. (1986). Assessing national data on education. *Educational Evaluation & Policy Analysis, 8,* 1–16.

Wiersema, B., Loftin, C., & McDowall, D. (2000). A comparison of supplementary homicide reports and national vital statistics system homicide estimates for U.S. counties. *Homicide Studies, 4,* 317–340.

Wilks, S. S. (1951). Undergraduate statistical education. *Journal of the American Statistical Association, 46*(253), 1–18.

Willms, J. D., & Kerckhoff, A. (1995). The challenge of developing new educational indicators. *Educational Evaluation and Policy Analysis, 17,* 113–131.

Wirt, J. et al. (2004). *The condition of education 2004* (NCES 2004–077). Washington, DC: U.S. Department of Education, National Center for Education Statistics.

Zvoch, K., & Stevens, J. (2008). Measuring and evaluating school performance: An investigation of status and growth-based achievement indicators. *Evaluation Review, 32,* 569–595.

Index

About the Author

Mike Planty received his Ph.D. from the School of Public Affairs at American University. He is currently a statistician at the U.S. Department of Justice. He has been involved in the design and analysis of large-scale household and school-based surveys in the areas of education and criminal justice. His research interests have focused on the sociology of education in high schools, measurement of crime and victimization, and issues related to statistical literacy.

Deven Carlson is a Ph.D. candidate in political science at the University of Wisconsin–Madison. He is a graduate fellow in the Interdisciplinary Training Program in Education Sciences and a graduate affiliate of the Institute for Research on Poverty. His research interests include education policy, housing policy, policy evaluation, and political participation.